Sheila M Hutchings is a lady of 55 years of age, living in a
bungalow with her cat Freddie in a Dawlish country lane,
having been a widow for the last six and a half years.

To Jane, my dearest daughter, for her love, support and encouragement always, but especially during lockdown.

Sheila M Hutchings

HUMBLE BEGINNINGS

AUSTIN MACAULEY PUBLISHERS™

LONDON • CAMBRIDGE • NEW YORK • SHARJAH

A CIP catalogue record for this title is available from the British Library.

ISBN 9781528987547 (Paperback)
ISBN 9781528987554 (ePub e-book)

www.austinmacauley.com

First Published 2023
Austin Macauley Publishers Ltd®
1 Canada Square
Canary Wharf
London
E14 5AA

To my lovely daughter Jane, my granddaughters, Julia and Laura; and my loving, supportive family, both here and in the afterlife.

I was born on September 13, 1933 the fourth daughter of Violet and John (Jack) Melmoth at 1 Rock Cottages, Milbury Lane, Exminster, with a head of thick black fuzzy hair (so I was told by Mum). At the same time Dad won the football pools (a fairly small amount – I believe the only time he ever won something after a lifetime of trying!) and bought Mum a Singer Sewing Machine which proved to be a blessing to all of us at various times.

Dad was 6'2" and Mum 5'3", the long and the short of it, but they were wonderful parents. They were very proud of us all as we were of them. Dad played terrific games with us and my most vivid memory is waiting for him to come home from work, when we were very young, and queuing up to have a 'walk' up his long body by holding his hands and turning a somersault at the end. How we screamed and loved it.

I also remember riding on his bike (on the crossbar) and going with him at an early age when he visited people to repair their kettle, iron, radio etc. Although he worked at the Exminster Mental Hospital as an electrical engineer (he retired as the Chief Electrical Engineer), he would also help anyone who had problems with their electrical appliances.

If Dad was the mainstay of the family; Mum was the anchor. She was a wonderful Mother and Nurse – it was always a pleasure to be ill and have Mum wait on you hand, foot and finger – and she could always find a book or puzzle left over from Christmas to make you forget your ailments.

Mum left school at 14 and became a 'chippy' (waitress) in Colsons (Frasers now) where she met Uncle Harry, who was her boyfriend for a time until she met his brother (our dad – an electrician by trade) who snapped her up and they got married about 1915. She had beautiful handwriting, was a very good speller and an expert at writing letters which we all took advantage of when applying for jobs etc. She also had a wonderful sense of humour and for the most part was happy with her lot, but she was the boss and ruled the roost (most times), but we all knew when we stepped out of line by her expression (and a clip on the ear if it was warranted!) We all loved her and were devastated when she died at an early age of 68 years, but luckily we were all grown up by then.

There were eight children in the family altogether. Five were born in Rock Cottages, Exminster – at the bottom of Milbury Lane (before Gissons or any of the other houses were even thought of) – Edna, Margaret, Barbara, Sheila and Gladys. Shirley was born when we moved to River View (at the bottom of the village) and then two boys, John and Mike, hallelujah and our family was complete, and we have always been very close, helping each other whenever we could.

Edna was the eldest of the family and as such was called upon many times to help with all of us – an absolute brick. She was especially kind to me (I know that several members of the family could say the same). When I was growing up (about 12 years old) she took me to the cinema where we saw Norman Wisdom in a lot of his films, *Rosemarie* (a wonderful film) and *The Way to the Stars* popular even today. Also to the local fairs and circuses, and introduced me to cafes and restaurants when we had tea in lovely little china cups. I have never forgotten it and never will be able to thank her enough for her love and kindness to me, especially in my early years.

Unfortunately, at seventeen years of age Edna caught typhoid whilst working in the kitchens at the Exminster Mental Hospital from one of the foreign workers employed there (as it was discovered much later on). We were all shocked when she was taken suddenly into hospital, and Lord Jesus was asked to work overtime to make her well again. Thank goodness our prayers were answered and she returned to us fully recovered. I remember a worried Mum and Dad returning one day from visiting her in Hospital saying how beautiful she looked lying there in bed, although she was so ill.

Our childhood at Milbury Lane was every child's dream, with fields and hedges surrounding us, a lovely stream to play in and of course, we had our own personal sweet shop (in our dreams) halfway up the Lane owned by a little old lady, dressed all in black, called Mrs Diamond (but Cocky by everyone behind her back) which sold sweets to die for – sherbet lemons, liquorice whirls, etc, and my favourite, jelly babies – you got more of those to the pound!

We also had the exclusive rights to the quarry (or so we thought) with lovely mossy banks covered in violets and primroses in the spring, and which had our own natural ski slope with a sledge (an old tin bath that we had found at the bottom of the quarry).

I was always getting into wars. One day, I tried to get the most from a lollipop I was sucking and pushed the stick into the roof of my mouth. The paramedics had to be called – Mum and Dad with his old trusty steed (his bicycle) – who placed me on the crossbar and pedalled furiously up to the Exminster Mental Hospital (the Asylum) for a doctor to treat me. Who needed the A&E?

I don't know what we would have done without Dad's bike. Several of us had accidents of one sort or the other. All the Doctors knew Dad (he was very popular with everybody) and were only too pleased to give us emergency treatment when necessary.

I remember I cut my instep on a glass jar when playing and Dad wrapped a towel around my foot and hotfooted me (sorry) to the hospital where I had to have stitches without an anaesthetic because they were afraid there was still some glass in the wound. Ouch!

I attended the primary school and reportedly hated it as I left midday to come home. The truth is I had diarrhoea and had to run home and change my pants. I had a sympathetic teacher, though, Mrs Budd whom I loved dearly and who bought me sweets as a consolation!

As well as our antics in the quarry we used to walk to Green Ditch, near a sewage farm which grew beautiful Lupins (I can't think why) and have our picnics. (Obviously, we had no sense of smell when we were younger.) In the summer we were able to cross the marshes to Topsham, and also walk to Granddad's house (Dad's father's) at the bottom of the village – he was a retired Nurse at the hospital by then, having previously retired from the Grenadier Guards. He played the drums in the Band of the Grenadiers and I can always visualise him sitting in his chair when he came to see us in his later years, showing how he played them when marching in the Band, and reliving every moment.

He was also a dab hand with the scissors – he used to cut Edna, Margaret and Barbara's hair (I was too young thank goodness) and they hated it as they looked like escaped convicts when he finished, having cut off all their curls, but he was a lovely old man, very smart and well maintained, and we loved him dearly (well, some of us!!!)

We were also able to walk across the marshes to the Railway Station to catch the train to Dawlish Warren – wonderful days out. Dear Dad used to come in the sea with us and we had a super time. Dad had an old woollen swimsuit which he used to wear which had a small hole in the side. One day, rushing to catch the train, we left Dad's swimsuit on the rocks to dry. The next time we visited Dawlish Warren we found the suit – it was being worn by a buxom girl of about 12 years old – unfortunately the hole which had been quite small when Dad wore it, was now stretched to capacity and had moved from the side of the suit (when Dad had worn it) to her posterior – bluntly speaking to one of her buttocks. We laughed until we cried although, on Mum's kind but strict instructions, we had to hide our mirth until the 'dear girl' was out of sight.

We had a lovely Auntie Milly who was really Mum's cousin, and she took us for some super walks and played a lot of games with us in the fields. I remember that Mum bought a tiny little dolls pram for me at a Village Jumble Sale for my 8th birthday (Marg and Barb had been instructed to buy it for me before the sale began) and Auntie Milly made a mattress, pillow and some coverlets for it. She also bought me a small doll to go in the pram and knitted a beautiful complete outfit for the doll which fitted into a shoebox. I played with that doll, clothes and pram until it literally fell to pieces.

On another birthday she gave me a beautiful expanding bracelet made up of thirteen lozenge shaped pieces of Mother-of-Pearl with tiny pink rosebuds on each one. I treasured that bracelet and have never forgotten the pleasure she gave me on receiving such wonderful presents.

I used to stay with Auntie Milly and Uncle Ralph some weekends and we used to have sausages (Courtneys even in those days) and scrambled dried egg (both delicious). She used to keep all her perishable items – sausages, bacon, joints of meat etc – in a wire safe just outside the back door in the yard, (No refrigerators then). I don't know how we managed because all we had at home was a stone shelf in the larder! (That was when we moved to River View – I can't think what we had in Rock Cottages!!!)

Auntie Milly and Uncle Ralph had two lodgers who were switchboard operators and worked for British Telecoms (it wasn't called that then) and had to start at 7 am in the mornings. They were very kind to me and always made me feel welcome.

Auntie Milly also had a little dog called Nancy who was a dear little thing and didn't mind in the slightest when I used Auntie Milly's precious scales in my pretend shop to weigh her dog biscuits with a magic set of weights. How I was spoiled!

I know Auntie Milly once asked if she could adopt me but Mum was having none of that. I know that she was a Spiritualist but I think that Mum had asked her not to talk to me about it. I wish she had and I also wish now that I had spoken more to Uncle Ralph, Auntie Milly's husband. I remember him as a very kind man but he had been injured in World War I and sustained a broken jaw, which was very swollen and which I tried not to look at, making me tongue-tied when speaking to him as a result.

We used to visit our maternal grandparents who didn't live too far away from us in the village, and I used to see Granddad, who slept at Auntie Milly's sometimes when he worked on the trains at Tiverton Junction, I think he was a stoker on early turns in the mornings, and I saw him for a brief time then. Two aunties lived with them with their two children, and we did go and see them quite regularly in their little cottage with a funny little loo out the back that stunk to high heaven!

It had a scrubbed hard wooden seat with a bucket underneath, which we all used to sneer at but was jolly glad to use when the need arose! Goodness knows where the bucket was emptied but a horrible thought has suddenly occurred to me – Granddad used to grow the biggest cauliflowers in the village – and I used to love cauliflower cheese!!! Need I say more!!!

Our dear cousin June, who lived with Gran and Granddad and later married Bill, had a baby boy who died at birth, and the next day she herself passed. It was heart-breaking; our biggest tragedy in the family, and it took a long time for us all to get over it.

1940 was the year when the war really broke out. I remember Edna coming home from work to Rock Cottages saying in hushed tones that war had broken out and that everything was going to change. I still remember asking Dad what was going to change and he just said knowingly, 'We will just have to wait and see' (very helpful!) and we didn't have to wait too long! Everything did change, and rationing was the start – no more chocolate or sweets, or very little. It was then confirmed on our battery-driven wireless (which Dad miraculously kept going, replacing this and that valve and daring any of us to touch it). It was our lifeline – and we relied on Dad to keep it going as, apart from card playing, it was our one and only entertainment.

I remember one day seeing Dad in despair. He had been working on the wireless non-stop practically all day, trying this valve and that valve but to no avail. 'Well that's it, the damn thing won't work,' he said, and to me that was our death knell. (I was six years old I believe at the time.) What, no more wireless? We listened as a family to *Itma – Can I do you now Sir* to *Bandwagon* – a variety programme, and of course *In Town Tonight*, Talent Shows and a host of other wonderful programmes that we all thoroughly enjoyed and listened to avidly. What would we do if we could no longer listen to our faithful wireless?

Of course, I didn't realise at the time but valves cost money and dear Dad had very little of that to play with, with all us kids. There was no child allowance in those days, everybody had to fight for themselves, and Mum and Dad needed food for our mouths and there was very little left for entertainment, and a new replacement valve was out of the question.

Well, there was only one thing for it and I knew what to do. I would ask Lord Jesus to help us. I had tried it once before and it worked – when the baby was ill and I prayed for her to get better, and she did – so it was sure to work this time, and so I got down at the side of the bed and prayed and prayed, asking Him to make our wireless work again, and that if He did I would be a good girl for the rest of my life, or knowing

16

me, well perhaps the rest of the day. Anyway, I was convinced that my prayers were going to be answered.

Dad was reading the paper – he had given up on the wireless which was pushed to one side of the table. I went to him. 'Dad, Dad, please try the wireless one more time. It will be awful if we haven't got a wireless to listen to.' Dad shook his head resignedly but, to please me, rose from his chair and went to the wireless again, ready to satisfy me that it was useless, a waste of time to try. I don't think he actually kicked the table leg but he sat down again and started to fiddle with the knobs in desperation. 'Look she, it's not going to work, and it's had it' and then all of a sudden the wireless let out a squawk (as it used to before it was tuned in) and then we heard sweet music echoing forth. 'Well,' he said, 'I never did.' No, he didn't because Jesus did and I told him so, laughing and crying at the same time. 'Well it must be a miracle,' he said, scratching his head. I said it is Dad, it is, and it was, as far as I was concerned. We had our wireless back again.

Well, even after saying it was a miracle, dear Dad then set out to try to prove that the wireless was now working because he had left it to let the valve cool down, etc. etc. I didn't mind. Whatever he said I knew better. I had asked my friend to help and He had, so there and even to this day I know that it was a miracle!

After this the wireless worked perfectly over the years with, I suspect, many new valves to help it behave, and when Luxemburg, a new channel, arrived a bit later we girls were in our seventh heaven – we were able to buy the words to all the popular songs at that time and had great fun duetting with all the singing 'greats'.

I say the only entertainment was the wireless but Dad had managed to buy a cinematograph (which needed another valve to work it) with masses of film on spools that had to be fed into it. Mum draped a white sheet over the pictures and voila, we had a screen. One night the fire was burning very bright and Mum stood in front of it to block out the light. Unfortunately, her dress caught fire but Dad soon put it out with his quick thinking – throwing a vase of water (together with the flowers) to put it out. We had some lovely silent films with Felix the cat, Charlie Chaplin and many other favourites. We also had a record player and Mum had managed to buy a record of 'Sparky's Magic Piano' – I can still hear this voice saying, 'This is I, your Piano,' and we would spend hours listening to it.

We still continued to go to Dawlish Warren in the summer but now there was a lot of barbed wire on the top of the dunes to keep the 'jerries out' (as we used to say) and there was no ice-cream or any other luxuries for sale (of course, there never had been before but I am comparing with today) but we had our egg sandwiches and Mum's rock cakes and we were content.

We had some entertainment in the village of course. We went to church regularly on Sundays – Sunday school in the afternoons (on a hot day, I remember dreaming about a lovely ice-cold glass of water straight from the pump when I got home!) and then, when older, Church in the evenings. There was a boarding school for 'naughty boys' as we used to call them, and they went to church in the evenings – this was a big attraction for the older (naughty!) girls in the village!

We were very lucky to have a father who worked at the hospital and as a sideline he used to show films to the mentally ill patients once a week, and as a treat we were allowed to watch the films also, although Dad made very sure that we were kept at the back of the room out of the way of the patients, although I have to say, even living at Rock Cottages at a time when some patients were allowed to roam wherever they pleased, I am sure we were never at any risk. Dad even brought home some of his workmates for tea to meet us sometimes – old trusted patients from the hospital – dear old Fred was one of them whom we all got to know and love.

The films were really up-to-date and we enjoyed them immensely.

We also used to go to the Wesleyan Chapel to watch religious slides (which always frightened me a little with their strange faces), although the packets of Smiths crisps (with salt in blue twists of paper) we smuggled in to munch certainly helped to make our evening more acceptable but unfortunately I rather think, judging by the dirty looks that came our way from the organisers, it was us that were unacceptable!

Once the Americans joined in the war, an American base was situated in our quarry which really put paid to our adventures there. I still remember the trucks coming down the lane on the way to the quarry, full of these soldiers shouting at us children and grabbing some of our apples on the high branches as they passed, and we became experts at catching the chewing gum, candy, chocolate bars etc that they threw at us, especially with sweet rationing in full spate at that time! We loved them for it – Anglo/American relations were certainly at their highest peak then in our part of the woods!

In 1940, we were fortunate to be offered a Council House at River View in the road where Granddad Melmoth lived.

Sadly, Dad's mother Frances had died at the time Mum and Dad married – Granddad had insisted that the wedding still went ahead. Much later he met a French governess, Granny Rose, and married her. I remember her as being a bit starchy but always very kind and welcoming when we called to see Granddad, who had the loveliest garden with small box hedges and lovely little paths leading off. I thought it was fairyland. He also had a tree on the side of his house which grew beautiful peaches; he really had very green fingers!!! He also grafted several roses on to one stem – he was so clever.

When Granny Rose died after a short illness, Auntie Dot Dad's sister and Uncle Stan came to live with Granddad together with Pauline (the same age as Glad), their little daughter. Uncle Stan was a RAF Navigator in the War and had a terrific sense of humour, and would keep us in fits with all his tales of the war. (I am sure he made half of them up but we all loved them and him just the same.)

From time to time also our uncle (Dad's brother) and his wife used to come down to Devon for holidays, with their two boys, and I was very lucky to spend a lovely holiday with them in Beckingham, Kent, when they took me to see 'Oklahoma' in Drury Lane, my very first musical, with Howard Keele as the leading man. We had to sit on little stools in a long queue to get seats but we managed it, and it all added to the experience!

My Uncle also took me to the department store where he worked, and treated me to a new coat. I loved him forever after that, although he never let me forget that I used the sugar dispenser on the train when eating a meal and had to pretend that I liked sugar with my fish ever after – well, I was different, anyone can have salt!!!

It was heaven living at River View. We had electricity, were able to have baths and had more space to sleep and hang our clothes, but how I missed the cosiness of Rock Cottage. By then Shirley had arrived, a beautiful little girl whom everybody loved, and I was nine when Johnny was born (1942) and loved him to bits. He was the only boy (with six sisters). Michael, (a darling little boy whom we all adored), came after him in 1952. Johnny was like a little angel. I entered him in a baby competition at our village fete and he won first prize, and I am sure there wasn't a more proud family than ours in Exminster that day.

Unfortunately, when he was about four years old he had a very bad accident with the kettle. I am afraid our cat jumped from his arms and pulled the kettle on top of him, scalding him very badly. Poor Mum was demented but thanks to one of our neighbours who was a Nurse, he was rushed to hospital and given emergency treatment. (Once again, Lord Jesus was petitioned, and once again He answered our prayers!) Thank goodness Johnny's face was not marked in any way (he grew up to be a very handsome young man) but he had a lot of scarring on his dear chest.

All through our childhood we had animals of some sort. We always had cats, and Dad kept rabbits (Blue Beverans, Chinchillas, Angoras, Brown Havanas, etc., etc.,) in the war for food and for showing. I remember going to several rabbit shows with Dad in Exeter and he often used to win the first prize. He was also secretary of the local rabbit show committee when it was held in the Victory Hall, and I often used to accompany him. We had several rabbit skins that we had cured and Mum made gloves for us out of them. Very fashionable and very acceptable in the war!

We had a dear sheepdog type of dog, Sandy, but unfortunately he had wanderlust (or was looking for a girlfriend) and got killed on the road. We were all devastated. I remember just after we lost him, walking along the street in Exeter sobbing my heart out, and thinking of all the times that I had shouted at him for being naughty and wished that I had looked after him better. If only I had known then what I know now, that he was probably walking along beside me, happy in his new life, and me not knowing that one day we would be together again, as with all our other animals!

We never returned to Milbury Lane again or visited our dear next-door neighbour Brightie who was very kind to us when we were small, and who made lovely jam tarts. She had two brothers whom we were allowed to call Uncle Jim and Uncle Gilbert. I am not sure what Uncle Jim did for a living but I know he paid Barb a penny every time she said 'bugger' (behind Mum's back of course!).

Barb had ginger hair and was very bright. Marg was also bright, and both were highly thought of by the headmaster, Mr Kelly, but they didn't like him. Kelly (our disrespectful name for him) had a terrible temper and would fly into a rage at the drop of a hat, (or a drop of anything really) and his face would go purple! – he would get arrested now for his behaviour! One morning he got so angry with a young lad (I forget why exactly) that he pulled him out in front of the class, tearing all the buttons off his shirt in the process. Imagine our delight when we saw the lad's father (a big bruiser of a man!) come striding into the school in the afternoon, bringing his son with him, together with the shirt and buttons and demanding that Kelly sew the buttons on immediately or take the consequences! With that ultimatum he turned on his heel and stumped off the premises.

Needless to say, Kelly didn't do anything to the shirt at all but took the offending article to the needlework teacher who had no option but to sit down, there and then, and sew the buttons back on, saving Kelly from the dire consequences that had been threatened, much to his embarrassment and to everyone else's glee.

It was always our favourite 'school' story in the family. The second favourite was when two inspectors visited the school and disappeared into a classroom, together with Kelly. That afternoon a funeral took place, and being the inquisitive creatures that we were, we all bounded up to the railings and watched as the procession passed by on its way to the church. You couldn't hear a pin drop, we were so engrossed. Well, it was so quiet that Kelly and the inspectors came out of the classroom to enquire what was up! When Kelly saw us all standing there quiet at the railings, he turned around to the inspectors and said, 'What about that, these wonderful children, showing such reverence,' and so saying he shouted to all of us 'You are very good children. For being so good you can take the rest of the day off' (He was trying to impress the inspectors no doubt). We all looked in astonishment – we were getting the rest of the day off – for what? It suddenly dawned on all of us that he had misread our curiosity but what did we care, we had the rest of the day off. Yippee, and anyway, who was going to tell him?

Back to Uncle Gilbert. He pushed a heavy wooden handcart around the village and sold fish which he collected from the train and dead rabbits, pheasants etc, or whatever he could get hold of from farms etc in the village (all legitimately, or so I like to think!) I am sure my mother was his best customer and I really do not know what we would have done without the many treats that turned up on his pushcart, and the lovely vegetables that Dad worked so hard to produce from his allotment (which he diligently attended every evening and weekend) but I have never tasted anything since as good as the meals that our mother produced from seemingly very little ingredients.

Margaret also played her part in filling our hungry mouths by working at the local fish and chip shop in the village and by bringing home all the leftovers which we devoured ravenously – gribbles, the odd faggot etc. etc. – delicious.

Of course, besides Uncle Gilbert making his rounds in the village, we had the local butcher and baker, and I shall never forget the milkman doling out milk into various receptacles from churns carried around in his private car – just imagine the state of it!!!

After leaving Milbury Lane we went for long walks to Nomansland, by way of Exminster Hill, using the pram to gather firewood (with the current baby riding on top) and had some lovely picnics with Auntie Jess, another sister of Mum's.

Auntie Dor (another of Mum's sisters) and Uncle Joe, who had been a Chief Petty Officer in the Navy in the War and was a great favourite of mine – he always looked so smart in his uniform – also lived in the village with their children and we often dropped in for a chat as we got older.

There was a big RAF Station very near to us in Exminster with radar, and Dad and Granddad (who were official wardens) were very nervous once the sirens went and the 'jerries' started coming over. In the beginning, we used to go under the stairs once the alarm went and I remember once Dad saying to Mum, 'That was a near thing,' and when we looked the next morning we saw some shrapnel embedded in our house where Dad and Granddad had been standing.

After using the space underneath the stairs during the raids, the government provided us with a Morrison shelter – a big steel table with mesh sides. Mum used to keep blankets in there and it was very comfortable although I think nearly all of us suffered from sore heads when the sirens went and we rushed to get in.

It was quite a frightening time looking back and the only bright side that I can remember is going to an 'Ensa' Concert in the RAF Camp once a week when we enjoyed seeing some quite famous celebrities entertaining the troops (and us).

At the age of 11 years I was diagnosed by the school doctor (I can't thank her enough) as having curvature of the spine, (I was lucky, poor Margaret had it also but was never diagnosed or treated) and I suffered the ordeal of being in a plaster cast from my collar-bone to the tops of my legs for a year, (The boys at school had great fun knocking on my plaster cast, they said to see if there was anybody in – there was occasionally when I wasn't off on one of my daydreams) and a steel jacket for another year, but it did the trick, together with the ballet and tap dancing classes Glad, Shirley and I attended every week, under sufferance. The doctor had said that I needed exercise; swimming was out of the question (living in Exminster away from the local swimming baths), so dancing classes it had to be. (In the event we visited Exeter every week so we could have easily attended the baths!) Mum insisted on Gladys and Shirley also attending the classes as she said she would not just pay for me, they must also attend – no favouritism allowed!

Dear Mum (what a wonderful woman I now realise in my adult life) had to take me to the Orthopaedic Hospital every month as by then I was developing rapidly and had to have pieces cut out as well as pieces let in. (Not a pretty sight!) She used to have a knitting needle and insert it in the top of the jacket to alleviate the itching with talc. The high spot of our month was to see Dr Capener, who was a young German doctor (he now has a ward named after him in the R.D&E,) He was a really nice man and used to call me his 'sausage' (looking back he should have called me his 'frankfurter' – I'm glad he didn't – that sounds quite rude! – but it must have been very difficult for him being a German living in England at that time.

The war ended in 1945 and I remember that everybody was happy. Mr Churchill, the Prime Minister, and then the King, gave speeches, and Dad insisted that we all sit down and listen. Everywhere you went people were laughing and slapping each other on the back. It was wonderful and then we had a street party and everyone contributed. It was a joyous time.

1947. Life at River View, after the war, was a happy time, as I remember. On Saturday nights, we had to show Mum and Dad what we had learnt at the dance lessons we had attended that day – this was for us to remember our steps for any dancing displays we would be called upon to take part in, and also to ensure that Mum's money was not wasted! Tap dancing in the morning (we used to buy fish and chips for our lunch and take them to eat in a friend's home) ready for ballet classes in the afternoon. (Glad was actually very good at ballet and passed several grades.) Unfortunately, Saturday nights were the nights that the lads (Ken and Roy) came to collect Margaret and Barbara for their nights out, (Edna had flown the nest by then) and they mocked us unmercifully, usually Roy, telling us to keep our heads up, shoulders back and to lift our legs higher, and usually banging a walking stick on the floor to keep in tune with the music produced by Ken on his mouth organ. We all stuck our tongues out at them and made other obscene gestures, behind Mum's back, of course, but actually it was great fun, and when we got older we always remembered those 'jam' sessions long after the dancing lessons had ceased (two and a half years' duration) and we had outgrown our moments of fame. We were called 'The Trio' dancing and singing to 'putting on the ritz' with me in long trousers and a blouse and the two girls in frilly dresses at the Phyllis Scanes Dancing Displays at the popular Theatre Royal. We went on to attend several displays – Glad doing a ballet dance and Shirley and I tap dancing.

The Theatre was situated in the heart of Exeter. It was a little way back from the main street (just down from the Castle) and, if it was still in being would face between John Lewis on the right and Waterstones on the left. It was a very old theatre (Dad told us that he and Mum used to sit up in the "gods" to watch all the wonderful variety shows for sixpence when they were courting). Jane and I also went to see The Beatles in the ABC Cinema when she was in her teens (sadly this is now gone but was not very far from the theatre) on one of the rare occasions they visited Exeter.

None of us were selected to take the 11+ exam and I never really knew if we were ever offered the chance, but in any case with five of us by then (the younger ones wouldn't have

27

been in our age group), it would have been impossible (the uniforms alone being out of the question), although I am sure that we would all have stood a good chance when comparing us with the other children who did pass, especially now, looking back at what we achieved in our later lives.

Edna who was a professional cook in her own right, in charge of the catering at a large school, Margaret who eventually joined me at the Ministry and made a name for herself whilst working for the Chief Veterinary Officer, Barb who became a Senior Mental Health Nurse, Glad, who was a forerunner in mastering the computer in her job and was second in command when she worked for the comptometer department at Starcross Hospital, (she later managed the Stowey Arms in Exminster with her husband Derek, and another public house in Exeter on her own) and Shirley, who became a supervisor for a large wholesale food outlet, together with other managerial roles in her later life. John was an expert carpenter, and became a Planning Manager, responsible for the maintenance of the RD and E. and other local hospitals, and Mike, who attained the post of Site Manager and Assessor for a large building firm in Exeter – so we all did pretty well for ourselves, and all owned our own homes.

I, like Glad (and eventually Shirley, John and Mike) left the primary school and attended the Dawlish Secondary Modern School where I was fortunate to be placed in the 'A' Stream. The head teacher, Mr Gempton, helped me enormously and I had wonderful teachers, and I remember a Miss Cousins, in particular, who really encouraged me, and eventually at 14yrs, I passed an exam to attend a business course taking shorthand, typing, accountancy, English and maths at the Torquay Technical College for three years, and held my own in spelling, mental arithmetic etc. I travelled on the train between Exminster and Torre Station with a season ticket, and will always be grateful to Edna, Margaret and Barbara for helping me financially throughout those years, and this course stood me in good stead for my career when I eventually joined the staff of the Ministry of Agriculture.

I made many good friends whilst at the tech, including a lovely girl in my class (Norma), very tiny and a marvellous athlete, who joined a ballet group in the end and became a famous ballet dancer. She had an older sister and I got on very well with them all. They lived in a beautiful flat at the top of Torquay, and they took me under their wing, treating me like one of the family, and taking me out for lovely meals and other happy events. They were the ones who advised me to contact the education committee as I believe their father had seen an advertisement in the paper asking for shorthand typists. I have a lot to thank them for! They were lovely people but sadly, living so far away in Exeter, and there were no such things as mobiles in those days, inevitably we lost touch.

During this time, I sometimes stayed weekends with a dear friend (Hilda) at Torquay, and spent many happy hours with her and her father in their little shop in St Marychurch, and also staying on her mother's farm in a little village near Kingsbridge. One weekend, my friend said she wanted to go to a concert in a Ballroom in Torquay and would I go with her. The entrance fee wasn't very much so I agreed but when we got inside I found that it was a talent competition and they asked for volunteers. I said I would sing 'The Home-Coming Waltz', and eventually won the first prize. (There were twelve competitors.) This was a lovely time for me and I was offered a chance to sing with a dance band, going around the villages but, after trying it for a few times and being very shy (I was only sixteen), I decided that that life was not for me and gave it up to concentrate on my studies.

1949. Whilst at the Torquay Technical College (or South Devon Technical College to give it its official title), darling Mum and Edna entered me in the Exminster Carnival Queen competition. No, it was not for my good looks, it was for the one who collected the most money. They went to all the pubs and clubs around the village and even went to Topsham, and, thanks to them and their wonderful efforts in raising £30, I became the Carnival Queen with a boy attendant and three girls and had a lovely time. Dad rigged up a crown on our council house which lit up (well most of the time) and Mum did us all proud by making various outfits for the family and hiring a lorry for a tableau. Johnny was 'Nature Boy', Fred (our cousin) and Shirley were 'Darby and Joan', Barb was a mermaid (the tail kept falling off) and Glad was a bathing belle, although I think she was scheduled to carry a birdcage whilst singing 'My old man said follow the van', but she wasn't having any of that, thank you very much!

The carnival was a huge success with over 200 tableaux, the 'naughty boys' accompanying all the tableaux with burning tins on sticks (the safety chaps would have a field day today) but it was good fun for four days with a crowning ceremony in the victory hall to begin with and a concert, and a dance at the end of it, with me sitting in state on a throne in a beautiful (it was) pink crinoline dress and clutching arum lilies in my arms. Because of the success of the carnival and us raising such vast amounts, the village gained more swings and roundabouts for the sports field, and, even more important – wait for it – a bigger area of tarmac for the picnic tables!

I must now mention the wonderful pantomimes that we were privileged to be part of, as children of staff, at the Exminster Hospital, and even dear Dad, when he was able, always enjoyed his annual appearance, and so the dancing came in very handy when we were enlisted in the chorus line, together with Barb and Roy, her husband. The cast of the pantomimes were always very good, especially the Dame who was a smashing chap, and could keep us all in fits of laughter (very professional), and of course the nurses, sisters and doctors played their parts in being really good sports.

The Hospital also held a sports day for the staff and patients and this was a jolly good day out – it had hoopla stalls, and a game involving horse racing (I loved it and won quite a bit of money on it one year – the lever kept getting stuck on the same number – but it was good fun and even Barb thoroughly enjoyed it, with her beautiful long red hair streaming out behind her, when winning the staff's bicycle race!

It was about this time that we were the proud owners of a telephone (the only one in the street) because Dad was on emergency call-out as a fireman at the hospital, and this was a very useful addition to our home as we were able to accept and make calls, under strict supervision from Mum who furnished us with a coin box in the end to discourage us from any unnecessary usage! We younger girls thought it was very posh to have our own line, which I suppose it was at that time when telephones were in short supply!

1950. This was the year when I finished my business course, having taken the final exam, and, equipped with the necessary certificate, applied to the Devon County Education Committee for a post as shorthand typist at Larkbeare (the old Judges Lodgings), and was lucky enough to be accepted. I think I was getting £2.50 a week! The typing pool was situated in the attic (I can't believe it looking back) and I thoroughly enjoyed my job in the two years I was with them, but left in 1952 to seek a job with more career prospects, and applied to an insurance company as a clerk/shorthand typist, in the middle of Exeter which enabled me to walk through the town and see all the shops (a novelty for me after living in a village all my life).

Looking back, I did not enjoy this job very much as there was very little training, and I had to learn as I went along, but nothing disastrous happened (I don't think) and I luckily got on well with the staff, especially a girl whom I became very friendly with and who eventually invited me to her home for tea where I met her brother Jack. She had warned me that he was a bit of a rogue – they didn't get on very well – and when Jack turned out to be a good-looking chap and very personable (he had a car – an Austin 7 as well as a motor bike!) he was a very pleasant surprise. He also turned out to be very good at his job. He was an Engineer at a large engineering firm in Exeter and was very popular with all the chaps he worked with, helping them whenever they got stuck with any problems. (I was told this by a friend he worked with for several years.)

After a time Jack and I became friendly and the rest is history. Jack's sister eventually emigrated to Canada and had a lovely life, marrying a Canadian and having three children. She was always very generous and used to send us lovely parcels with jewellery and clothing for me and lovely little dresses for Jane.

Jack and I became engaged and married on the 19th December, 1953. I left the insurance company and Jane was born the following year, and we lived happily with Jack's mother Margery until our bungalow was built in 1955, in Whipton, Exeter for the princely sum of £1200. We managed to buy this on mortgage and by Jack putting down the deposit by selling his beautiful BSA star twin motor-bike. I used to love riding pillion on the back, and remember going for a holiday with Margaret and Ken one year, and, with our hearts in our mouths, seeing our beautiful bike being lifted high up in the air by a crane when we caught the ferry and landed in the Isle of Wight.

Now, I must tell you about my second mum. Jack's mum was the dearest kindest person you could ever wish to meet. She was in her late fifties when she welcomed me into her home for the first time. Jack and I had just got married and I was very green at anything to do with housework and cooking so when I (and eventually Jane) joined Jack and his mother in their bungalow, (which incidentally she had helped to build from scratch with her late husband) funnily enough I enjoyed assisting her with all the household chores (my own dear mum had a job to get me to even wash the dishes at home!) as well as using the vegetables in the garden and learning to make good tasty meals out of a pound of mince, and anything else that was cheaply to hand. I remember especially that she was very insistent that I use Pyrex dishes for cooking as she maintained that cooking in plastic bags, or anything plastic was cancer inducing!

Every young girl, newlywed, should have a dear mother-in-law as I did to teach her the ropes, never criticising and always ready to give her approval of a job well done. I learnt how to cook and to keep house in the easiest and best possible way, and to be happy at the same time, and I have never ever forgotten her love and kindness to me and to Jane. She was always ready to babysit at any time, and adored Jane right from the start, and always said that she was the best thing that had ever happened to her.

Now, thinking about it, I think the worst thing that ever happened to her was when she purchased a goat – or perhaps I should say, that happened to all of us! She said she had always wanted a 'billie' to keep the grass down! (It would have been so much easier if she had settled for a ride-on and hired a Billie to ride it!) Well, we managed to buy a goat from a farmer who lived not very far from where we live now, and named him George. This goat turned out to be a 'nanny' when unexpectedly we received a 'phone call from Mum at seven o'clock one morning to say that George was now Georgina and was having a 'baby'!

Now, Georgina had taken a fancy to Mum's washing hanging on the line, namely her unmentionables, tearing them off the line for a past-time – in fact she was more partial to them than she was to the grass. Jack eventually shifted the clothes line to the bottom of the garden, to put Mum's delectable undies (according to Georgina) out of her reach!

Now all of this was dwarfed by the fact that, shortly after we had the disastrous morning call telling us that our new addition to the family was a female and not a male, and giving the 'baby' away to a local farmer – we soon decided that one goat was more than enough – we had the added problem of having to milk Georgina, and Jack and I nearly came to blows when Jack said that I would make a far better milk-maid than he would a milk-boy, and refused to take on the job. We compromised – I would do the milking if he would produce a method of keeping Georgina in one place to enable me to be able to do the necessary – so, in the end, I had a go, after Jack had fixed up a stall for Georgina to be secured – or so he thought!

Well, after some time we managed to 'persuade' Georgina to enter the stall that Jack had made for the purpose and I, armed with a pail and a small stool, proceeded to have a go. Unfortunately, Georgina saw me coming and after being securely fastened to the stall, as Jack had thought, she managed to turn completely around and faced the other way. Well, I now had to change my position – she wasn't going to get the better of me – and I had another go, and eventually managed to coax a few drops into the pail before she decided she wanted a change of scenery once again and turned around once more, but this time knocked the stool from under me, kicking the bucket with the few drops of precious milk that I had gingerly extracted, (and held lovingly by Mum) flying skywards.

Well, we all had a good laugh but decided there and then that enough was enough and that Georgina would have to go, but imagine our delight and surprise when Mum rang us early the next morning to say that she had successfully milked Georgina and that she (Mum not Georgina) was sat in her kitchen drinking the 'nectar from the gods' (as she put it) onto her cornflakes.

Mum became very fond of Georgina (funnily enough) and kept her for some time after our never-to-be forgotten milking adventure, but in the end I think it was a relief for all concerned to see her go. We never really found out how Mum mastered the art of milking and I for one was not particularly interested in finding out (I wonder why) and we were not really sorry to see that part of the garden empty when next we visited!

But I am 'jumping the gun'. We moved to Brookside Crescent (our lovely two-bed roomed semi-detached bungalow, with a little neat garden front and back) in February 1955, when Jane was ten months old. I suppose you could say that I had plenty of training to be able to rear my own child and in a way, I did, there had been plenty of babies to change their nappies and feed many times at home with the family, but nothing prepared me for the feeling of helplessness I first experienced when coping with the everyday problems that beset me as a young mother having to look after a baby completely on my own. Was the water too hot for her bath? Was the milk too hot in her bottle? Was she sleeping too long, etc., etc., and I began to realise just how spoilt I had been, having had a wonderful mother-in-Law who shared all the responsibilities of the baby and also the many jobs that needed doing in the household, (not to mention the cooking) and it came as a bit of a shock when I realised that I was now on my own.

I remember one night that Jack and I were so worried about the baby, who had a terrible 'crouping' cough that had just begun, that I telephoned the doctor (a locum). He was extremely helpful and after treating her as he had advised, we settled down to our evening meal when the doorbell rang and there on the doorstep was this tall, immaculately dressed man who introduced himself as the doctor that I had previously spoken to. He came in and examined the baby and said that he was at a dinner but felt that he had to come and satisfy himself that she was alright as I had sounded so worried on the telephone. Poor man, I had ruined his night and said so, but he assured me that he had eaten his meal and that he could now return home with a clear conscience. What a lovely man and a wonderful doctor and I have never forgotten him!

As well as looking after the baby I had to prepare the evening meal for us (Jack and I – he took sandwiches for lunch) and as well as all the other clothes to wash, Jack needed a clean pair of dungarees every other week – he worked for an engineering firm, and working with all the machinery got very dirty. Jane's nappies also had to be boiled and hung out to dry – no throw-aways then. Thank goodness we had already purchased an electric boiler which Jack had installed in one of our little outhouses at the back of the bungalow. The steam used to billow out the door when I got it going – and I was really proud to see Jane's nappies brilliantly white and flapping merrily on the line.

Well, I soon got used to my new life and in time took it all in my stride, and enjoyed being on my own (with my faithful radio to keep me company).

When we moved in we had very little furniture to call our own but were very lucky to receive some pieces of furniture that Jack's mother had given us, including a lovely antique round table with lion legs – yes, claws and all! It was a lovely table but I couldn't wait to replace it with a modern table and four dining room chairs which didn't take up so much room. What an ungrateful wretch! Looking back on it now I wish that I had appreciated it more, although I did give it a good polish from time to time (especially when Mum visited).

Mum had also given us an old dresser for the kitchen and two kitchen chairs which Jack and I painted in a lovely blue, with oilcloth to match on the table and dresser, blue linoleum for the floor and blue check curtains at the window. It was a lovely cosy little kitchen and I loved it, even more, I think, than the one we replaced it with when we took out the larder to make it bigger, and modernised it with a new fitted kitchen.

My dear mum gave us some curtains for the two windows at the front of the bungalow.

We managed to buy a new bed and mattress and I spent a lot of my time going to various second-hand furniture auctions (with Mum babysitting). I remember I bought an old sofa (very comfortable) which we were always going to have recovered but never got around to it (or I suppose we couldn't afford to have it done) but the day did eventually arrive when I persuaded Jack to buy a dining room suite on hire purchase (much against his will) after he had decorated the lounge (this was Jack's first attempt but he really excelled himself). When this was paid off we bought two armchairs – there was no room for a three-piece suite. We then decorated our bedroom, after we had paid the last instalment on our previous purchases, and bought a lovely bedroom suite in oak, together with long lilac curtains and a light grey carpet.

We were so proud of our efforts (and rightly so, the bungalow looked lovely) especially after we replaced Jane's little cot with a single bed and a very useful little wardrobe when she was older.

We soon settled down to family life. We had a lovely neighbour who used to live in a house behind us. She was in her thirties and had two children and her husband was a very kind man who was a horticulturist and a teacher in a nearby approved school, and gave me some very good gardening tips, which I have been able to use on all our gardens that we have possessed over the years, and I shall always be grateful to him. His wife was a very good friend to me and helped me immensely in many ways on how to housekeep and look after the baby. (I was only 21 years old after all).

There was one thing that I wasn't quite so pleased to remember my neighbours by. They had a terrier called Sheila. (Yes I took a dim view of her having my name too, but I couldn't grumble, she was there before me after all!) but I took a really, really dim view of her when she visited our bungalow one day by the front door and left by the back, taking my lovely roast leg-of-lamb (resting on the dresser) in its mouth on the way out! Yes, they could have trained her better than that – they should have made her return it! She was my least favourite dog after that!

We went for some lovely walks around all the lanes, and even going for picnics in a field that has now a big school built on it with a housing estate surrounding it, and there was one field near us that was used every year for the Devon County Show, held on three days in May. I used to love to attend on one of the days and see all the animals in the show ring and the horses being put through their paces in the jumping arena. When I was employed later on by MAFF I used to organise the staff's refreshment tent every year for the three days and I loved it.

We also had some neighbours living opposite who owned a family grocery store and used to call for my list and then deliver my order the following day. They were lovely people with a beautiful garden, four times the size of ours which kept them busy mornings and evenings. I remember thinking thank goodness our garden is small and manageable – I didn't ever imagine that one day I would have one that would be over two acres in size and extremely unmanageable at times!

Jane was a happy baby, very content, and grew into a lovely child. I loved her dearly and we had a lovely time together, and we still do and have been great companions all our lives! Jack and I used to tease her and ask her who she loved the most and her stock reply was always 'I love you boff', and I shall never forget the day when it snowed and I went into her bedroom and pulled back the curtains and said, 'Look Jane, look at the snow darling.' And she replied, 'Oh! Thank you Mummy.'

We visited Jack's Mum regularly as she was now on her own. She must have been quite lonely but she never complained!

When we had nights out with friends, Jane stayed with Mum (they got on so well) and of course, as Mum was in her late fifties, she needed help with the garden and we often used to go out at weekends when Jack mowed the lawn for her etc.

One year the office went on a trip to the Chelsea Flower Show. I loved it and on the way back to the station I called into C & A, a big store in London, and bought Jane five beautiful little dresses in their sale. I was very naughty because when I got home I woke her up – I was so excited to show her the dresses – I don't think she slept very well that night – what a naughty Mother!

Jane was about nine years old when we purchased a lovely little budgie who we named Buddy but had to quickly change it to Budelina because it laid an egg (I believe that was the reason!). We tried hard to get her to talk but she wasn't having any. Jane was very fond of her and used to let her out of her cage sometimes which was fine, but one day, when she was busy with her homework, Budelina started to fly dangerously near to an open window Jane had forgotten to close. She raced after it and managed to catch her, thank goodness – we would have broken our hearts if she had managed to escape – but unfortunately Jane was holding her fountain pen in her hand at the time and the ink went all over a wall that Jack had recently wallpapered. As the stain didn't quite fit in with the pattern of the wallpaper – in fact it stuck out like a sore thumb – he had to redo the wall all over again! He wasn't best pleased but I am glad to say that Budelina remained with us for a few more years, with no more mishaps, on Jane's part or hers.

We used to cover Budelina with a tablecloth at night – I still have it in the drawer with our other cloths, Persil white, but I can never bring myself to use it – I can still see it draped over the cage!

After Budelina we obtained a little ginger kitten (I am not quite sure from where) but he was beautiful and developed into a super cat (we named him Sandy) that we all loved. We had him all through Jane's childhood and he died at the grand old age of nineteen years, at Cherry Tree Close, the lovely upside-down house that we moved to after we left Brookside Crescent.

We had lovely Christmases. I remember once that we bought Jane a beautiful new doll's pram (a miniature silver cross model in grey) with a big doll to go in it; we were so pleased to be able to afford to buy them for her.

We used to go to Mum and Dad's on Christmas Day when most of us used to gather and enjoy a sumptuous feast, with Mum and Margaret excelling themselves with the cooking, after Dad had spent hours preparing all the vegetables. We all joined in even if it was only to do the washing-up. Mum always made the Christmas cake and Christmas puddings and usually it was necessary to have two sittings for lunch when the little ones used to have their meals first with the older ones having theirs after returning from the local pub! How we enjoyed it, especially when we were all grown up and brought our own little ones to the party. The Christmas tea was another feast and supper was something we all looked forward to, with Mum's chutney and pickles to go with the cold turkey and ham. Wonderful Christmases. How lucky we were, especially having Mum present. How we missed her when she wasn't!

John and Sue, and Jack and I purchased a hut at Dawlish Warren. We bought it together – it cost us £75.00 each couple and what fun we used to have when the whole family met up together, bringing various titbits to share, not forgetting Mum's contribution – lovely egg sandwiches and rock cakes that we all loved (as in our olden days!) Not many of us had cars but the ones who did crammed everybody in and the rest went by train. We all used to go in the sea (but not Dad – he left behind his swimming days – no suit perhaps!) – the summers always seemed perfect with Dad, enjoying himself in his deckchair under a shade, wearing his dabs (as we laughingly called them – his sandshoes size 12's) and Mum in her element with the children, picking up shells and making sandcastles. It was so good also at that time to see Jane, Lynne and Mike playing happily together – they were all about the same age. What a pity we cannot bottle happiness!

We didn't have a car for some time in our early days – Jack used his little motor bike to get to work – but we religiously saved up and were able to purchase our first

Austin, well, for the deposit at any rate, of a small black A30 when Jane was about six. When she got older we traded it in for an Austin Cambridge, a lovely smart car, black again. Jack used to do all the repairs and saved us pounds. Now that we had a car we were able to go on some lovely holidays. We went to Weymouth when Jane was about six and stayed in a boarding house for a week. We felt very grand!

By now, Jack had applied to the Chemistry Department at the Exeter University to work in their Research Labs to help in experiments and make lab equipment for the students. He was successful and right up to his retirement, was extremely happy in his work and very highly thought of. By this time, we had moved to Cherry Tree Close which was quite close to the University.

I remember we went to Goodrington when Jane was about seven years old and hired a caravan. It rained every day – it was a good job I took plenty of colouring books and board games with us but it didn't deter us from visiting the pier at Paignton and spending our pennies at the Penny Arcade, although it did put a stop to all Jane's favourite rides on the roundabout, caterpillar etc. As a consolation we bought her some roller skates!

I also remember when she was eight years old that we were invited to the wedding of a dear friend of mine, and at the reception we both went to the toilet, but unfortunately the lock on the door was faulty, but no matter, I held the door for her whilst she used the loo, and she reciprocated for me except that instead of holding the door secure, she decided that she wanted to show me a fancy dance step that she had just learned (which funnily enough I was not particularly interested in seeing as, strictly speaking, I was otherwise engaged) when suddenly she slipped, allowing the door to burst open to my horror, revealing me in all my glory, perched on the throne, to the surprise of all the ladies waiting patiently outside. I don't know who was the most embarrassed, me or the ladies, certainly not Jane who was laughing herself silly, but certainly me, trying to pull the door closed with one hand (nearly unseating myself in the process) and covering my dignity unsuccessfully with the other! I was not amused and it took me a long time to get over it. It wasn't a laughing matter, I tried to convince Jane, who begged to differ, saying, 'Dad, you should have seen the look on Mum's face!' when she was relating the sorry tale to him. Of course, I couldn't resist saying that it was not my face that I was particularly bothered about at that time, which was all the encouragement they needed to set them off again into peals of laughter. What a queer sense of humour we had!

We had some lovely holidays. One year we went to Wales to meet Jack's Welsh relatives – they made us very welcome and we were invited to go to a Miners' Club for an evening. We all played bingo, but what we couldn't understand was that the men went one way and the women went the other. They didn't mix – strange! This was going to be fun, or so we thought, but not a bit of it – nobody laughed – this was serious stuff. It certainly was eyes down and looking (intense concentration – I'm sure in our inexperience of the game we missed quite a few numbers), but once the game was over everyone was very sociable and friendly once more.

I am glad to say that no one spoke in their mother tongue – Welsh – so that you couldn't understand what they were saying, not like when we called for some petrol at a Welsh garage and not one person spoke to us in English – they chattered away in Welsh, they were so rude. I paid for the petrol in mime, pretending that I thought they didn't know any English!

We thoroughly enjoyed our trip to Lancashire to meet Jack's two cousins and their parents. They were lovely people – Jack's aunt and uncle made us very welcome and his cousins had a little daughter of about six (I believe Jane was about 12 years old then). Jack's cousin's husband was the headmaster of a comprehensive school, and proved to be a very interesting chap to talk to, and we visited some interesting places with them, Charlotte Bronte's home in Yorkshire being one of them. We also went to Blackpool but I am afraid the lights brought on a migraine for me and I had to leave rather hurriedly.

Our first holiday abroad was when Jane was about ten years old. We went to Spain and stayed in a hotel. That was a big adventure for all of us, but the best one was when we stayed in hotels in Florence, Venice and Rome for a week when she was about 14 years old. It was a coach trip but very interesting and very enjoyable, at the wonderful price of £24.00 each! Imagine!

Jack used to take us on some lovely car rides, and sometimes we would take Granny Rakestrow and Auntie Queen with us and call in for an ice-cream on the moors. That was a real treat for them. Jack was a good driver (he had actually driven the King when he visited Jack's Barracks when on his national service (Jack's, not the King's) and was chosen to be the King's chauffeur – what an honour).

Now rewind to 1956. When Jane was two years old, as Edna and I were both short of money, we agreed that I would find employment and pay her to look after Jane for me.

Thankfully Jane settled down very well with her, and enjoyed the company of Edna's daughter Lynne, who was a year or so older than her.

I applied for a job with the Ministry of Agriculture, Fisheries and Food as a shorthand typist and was lucky enough to be taken on by the Agricultural Land Service. After a year we were amalgamated into a typing pool for all the departments and eventually I became the second in command. I enjoyed this work but was then offered a chance to work for the head of the land service, which I did for another year, and then the secretary of the head of the divisional office left and I was asked to take her post. I then shared an office with two other secretaries and enjoyed eight happy years.

This was the time when Ivor (now my husband) applied for his job with the ministry and had an interview with my boss, and I had to receive all the applicants in a waiting room and supply them with coffee. He got the job.

Unfortunately, I found it very difficult to get to the office by 8.30 am by 'bus in the mornings, after dropping Jane off, but luckily, when I was talking to one of the Officers who lived nearby, he offered to give me a lift. This made things so much easier. He became a very good friend to us and, much to my delight, gave us advice on the garden which had very heavy clay soil, and soon our garden was one of the best in the crescent, and had the most loveliest standard roses. We had a gardening club in the office and held a flower show annually, and my roses walked off with the first prize at every show. We had a receptionist at the office who was blind (that wasn't because my roses always won the first prize!). Ray, a lovely chap, ran the club with his wife Eileen who also worked for the ministry, and were very keen gardeners (he used to work in the garden at night when preparing his produce for the shows!) We became very good friends and used to meet up after our retirement, with another couple, for lunch and social evenings.

When Jane was five she went to the Pinhoe Primary School and was looked after by our next-door neighbours who had moved to Pinhoe and had two children of their own going to the school. By a remarkable co-incidence Peggy, our next-door neighbour, met me in Dawlish one day, when we had moved there in the eighties. (It's certainly a small world!) Her husband had died and she was living on her own as her two children were now grown up and living away. We became friendly again (it was good to meet up) and I ended up helping her and giving her healing every week for the rest of her life.

1959. Jack and I eventually decided that we would like Jane to attend a private school in Exeter, she attended this school and did very well there before leaving to go to Exeter Technical College (now the Exeter College) where she studied law amongst other subjects.

When she left college Jane became an au pair in Paris where she was employed by an editor of the French magazine Marie Claire, looking after two little boys and learning French and teaching English in her spare time. (We paid her a surprise visit and enjoyed a short break with her in Paris) and whilst there Jane decided that she wanted to become a French teacher and after obtaining the necessary papers, applied to the Weymouth Teaching Training College where she was accepted and spent two happy years.

1966. When my boss was given promotion and moved to London I was also offered promotion as a clerical officer and moved into the subsidies section. From there I did various jobs and eventually was promoted to executive officer in charge of the subsidies section and after this, was made the personnel officer, working in the Establishment Section for seven years, and, amongst other duties, visiting and supervising the staff in the three area offices – Barnstaple, Tavistock and Totnes, etc. It was at this time that Margaret, my sister, joined the staff as a casual member of staff and became so proficient that one of the bosses requested that she be made his PA!

In 1973, I was instructed to take over the post of Finance Officer and I was very happy again in this post, having excellent staff to work with and enjoying working with figures, and also being in charge of the registry and map room. This post lasted for 11 years.

On the home front, Mum and I were very close, closer perhaps than I had ever guessed. One day when she and Dad were visiting Jack and I at Cherry Tree Close, Mum and I were looking out of our bedroom window, admiring the beautiful view – we often did this when Mum and Dad came to see us for a Sunday lunch – when she said, 'I have never ever told anybody this before but I know you will understand. When I was on the operating table, having my hernia operation, I had an "out of body experience." All at once I was in the air, floating down a large tunnel when I saw a very bright light at the end, which was drawing me to it, and I wanted to get to it so much and go through it – I didn't think of your father, you girls, the boys, no-one – I just wanted to go through that light, but then I heard a voice saying, "No Vi, it isn't your time yet, you must go back," and I felt a tremendous disappointment; I didn't want to go back, I wanted to stay and go through that light, but I wasn't allowed to. When I eventually woke in the recovery room I still had that disappointed feeling, as though I had suffered a great loss, but I will tell you something, I will never be afraid of dying ever again.'

Well, it was about two years later, when I was doing some ironing late at night waiting for Jack to come home from a film show he was giving at a hotel. He belonged to a team from the university, earning extra cash in his spare time (there were no videos or DVDs in those days) when all at once I felt as though the door had opened and someone had entered. I looked up and said, 'Hello you're back early,' thinking it was Jack returning, and I remember feeling a little foolish when I realised that no-one was there, but I looked at the clock to see if it was time for Jack to return and noticed that it was 11 o'clock, and then, all at once, it felt like the room was full of light, blindingly almost, and a feeling of great happiness so overwhelmed me that I sat down and began thinking of what had happened in my day to make me feel so happy. Well the feeling gradually faded, Jack came home and we went to bed but the next morning my dear brother John was on the doorstep to tell me that our dear mum had passed away the night before of a heart attack. She had been to a social evening at the hospital with Barbara, my sister, came home on the 11 o'clock 'bus and on walking up our road, had met a neighbour who asked her to telephone for an ambulance because her husband had had a stroke. Mum was hurrying to make the call when she fell and died in Dad's arms on the doorstep.

When we had Mum's funeral I was heartbroken, of course, but was so pleased that she had been able to come to me to let me know that she hadn't been afraid to die, and this carried me right through the service.

I tried to tell them all about Mum's experience on the operating table and her consequently visiting me when she died, but none of my family could really accept my story simply because, I believe, they were devastated to lose her, and didn't want to think about anything else. In any case, I am sure we must all personally experience spiritual matters ourselves to fully accept that they have actually happened, but I will never forget that wonderful feeling of happiness when she came to me on her passing, and it was through Mum that I eventually followed my spiritual pathway, but really I think her wonderful spiritual guidance started much earlier than that.

I have always been eternally grateful to her for so many things but I think the chief amongst them is for teaching us to say our prayers to God and Jesus every night. Saying them didn't make us saints – we were always falling out with one another – but the prayers taught us to stop and think of other people's wellbeing besides our own. Mum gave us stability in that one simple act, guiding us spiritually, just as my father created stability, teaching us right from wrong in our physical lives, as well as giving us love, and we had plenty of that. I passed on Mum's teaching to Jane.

As I have reported earlier, Mum discouraged my Auntie Milly from telling me about spiritualism because she believed that this was a religion that could lead to all sorts of wrong pathways. What a shame she didn't know the real truth – that for a start it isn't a religion but a way of life – to love thy neighbour as thyself, and follow all the commandments. What pathway can be better than that? If Auntie Milly had been allowed to explain this to me I might then have known, from an early age, about the angels that help us so much, that the scientists, surgeons, doctors, teachers etc. continue with their learning and carry out their experiments in heaven, once they have 'shuffled off this mortal coil'. These wise people are then able to pass on their wonderful results to receptive souls here on earth, as they helped with the vaccines recently and also important knowledge regarding 'Life after Death'. That life is so beautiful and much longer than this one, a sobering thought! How I wish that people who report someone's death would one day say 'Enjoy your new life' instead of saying 'rest in peace'. Will that day ever come – not in my lifetime but why?

I was always terrified about death. I cannot believe it now but I remember, as a very small child, looking in horror at the bowler hat that Dad used to keep on the top shelf in the wardrobe in our bedroom, frightened of its association to death, as I had seen Dad wear it at a funeral. I was frightened to death of it, and frightened OF death, I couldn't bear to look at it. I was so frightened that this life would cease and we would be no more and the thought appalled me – I loved all my family and friends and couldn't bear the thought of being without them, I would have been so relieved then to have known that life continued, that we didn't just go up in smoke, literally, but that we would go through a beautiful bright light into a much better life than this one – we would go back to our prime, lose all our aches and pains – and then we would be with all the dear ones that we had thought had been lost to us forever. When I did find out the truth it was as though a door had suddenly opened up for me and at last I could enjoy my life, without this constant fear hanging over me.

1976 was a year of upheaval for me in my private life. In 1974 I had met an office colleague (Ivor Hutchings) who was attending a meeting at the office (he remembered me as I had served him with coffee some twenty years ago when he attended the office for an interview for his present job). This was a momentous meeting as on re-acquaintance we discovered that we had a lot in common, especially concerning our spiritual lives. I was able to discuss my experience of Mum's passing with him, which I had never been able to with anyone else. Jack dismissed any talk of spirituality – sadly his father had died in his forties and anything involving death really frightened him (as it does a lot of people) – and after much heart-searching and a great deal of sadness as well as happiness, I eventually left Jack to live with Ivor in Paignton, who by then was divorced with a young daughter.

Leaving Jack was the hardest thing I have ever done in my life. Not only was I leaving Jack but I was leaving my darling daughter Jane, my dearest father and my dearest mother-in-law. I was also very ashamed that I had brought scandal on my own close family as well as to the ones I loved the most, but in the end it was inevitable. I can honestly say that was the worst time in my life, and yet the happiest once things got back on an even keel, but in my heart I knew that I had to do it, I loved Ivor, as he loved me, and I have never had any regrets for I was able to live my life to the fullest, and follow my spiritual pathway with someone who also held my beliefs, and after a short time I was able to renew my relationship with all my loved ones once again, to my relief. Jack also found a new partner.

Ivor was an adviser with the Ministry, having studied long and hard on various courses and taking a number of exams to become an agricultural engineer specialising in water, drainage and waste disposal, and he loved his work, visiting many farms in Devon and then in Somerset, taking charge of the ministry's Taunton Office on those duties for a spell when someone was taken ill at short notice.

Sadly, when only 19 years of age, Ivor contracted TB when his older brother Michael came home with it from the Burma Road after his spell on national service. Michael eventually died from it and Ivor spent two years getting over the disease (thankfully) and underwent rehabilitation, becoming a Horologist at St Loyes College for the disabled in Exeter where he was extremely happy and said he learnt a lot from his disabled colleagues. When he finished his course at St Loyes he worked for H Samuels (the Jewellers) at their Shops, first at Bristol and then Exeter for approximately five years. He was very proud of the letter of commendation they gave him when he left their employ.

When living in Paignton we resided in Ivor's lovely bungalow 'Thatcher View' (it had a beautiful sea view which I so missed) and spent three happy years before moving to a larger property, Millcroft Bungalow in Dawlish in 1979, after our Wedding in Oldway Mansions, Paignton, on June 16, and afterwards at the Redcliff Hotel.

Unfortunately, 'Millcroft Bungalow' had an agricultural tie attached to it which meant that if we wanted to live there (a) either Ivor or I would have to milk cows for a farmer (no – I'd had enough of the goat) look after chickens (no) etc. etc. or (b) it would have to be turned into a viable unit as the bungalow had been built for an agricultural worker. We opted for the viable unit but were advised by our solicitor to forget it as it would mean a lot of work to be able to satisfy the agricultural lease or tie. He was right and it was a lot of work but we ploughed on as Ivor could see that I had fallen in love with the bungalow and its lovely mature garden, and we spent a hard year attempting to satisfy all the conditions of the agricultural lease on paper before we actually put them all into practice, having purchased a further five acres from the previous owner to help to make it a viable unit. He was determined that we should buy Millcroft Bungalow and said that he was sure we would achieve great things by doing so. How right he was – did he have the foresight to see what wonderful spiritual work we would be carrying out by enabling us to purchase this beautiful property?

Moving into the bungalow and satisfying the conditions of the lease was in tandem with our work for the ministry, and it was quite an operation adjusting our workloads at weekends i.e. buying equipment to start our little enterprise, a cultivator, plastic tunnels to work in, sprays of every variety, chrysanthemum plugs and lastly young cider apple trees for the five acres of extra land we had purchased.

When we arrived on November 12, 1979 to begin our life at Millcroft Bungalow we had eight months to prepare before Jane and John's wedding in July 1980. They were to be married in the morning at the Exeter Registry Office, attend a lunch at a local hotel, receive a 'blessing' in the church in the afternoon followed by a reception at Millcroft Bungalow. Over 100 invitations were sent.

My dear sisters: Edna, Margaret, Barbara, Gladys and Shirley, together with the two Susans, our sisters-in-law, agreed to lend a hand with the buffet. Ivor managed to purchase some very good wine from the continent (his friend was in the trade) which was much cheaper than if we had obtained it locally. Of course we had barrels of beer as well and soft drinks. We also hired some glasses.

Mum and Dad's Wedding

Granny and Granddad Melmoth, Harry, Dot and our Dad Jack

*Edna, Margaret, Barbara, Sheila, Gladys and Pauline
(their Cousin) at Rock Cottages*

The Family with Auntie Millie playing in the fields

Auntie Millie, Uncle Ralph and their dog Nancy

John (Six months old) after winning the Baby Competition

Report on Exminster Carnival and the Crowning Ceremony

Sheila with Attendants

Carnival Tableau 1948

Exminster Hospital Pantomime

Edna's Wedding

Golden Wedding of Granny and Granddad Rakestrow

Family group Left to right: Margaret, Barbara, Sheila, Gladys Shirley, Dad. Mum with Baby Mike and Edna with Baby Lynne, John

Sheila and Jack's Wedding

The garden of our bungalow at Brookside Crescent

Proud Parents-Jack and Sheila with Jane

Mum Cairns with "Geraldine" the goat

Mummy's girl Jane with Sheila

Jane, Jack & Sheila on holiday in Weymouth

Mum, Dad, Sheila and Jane at Cherry Tree Close

Sheila and Ivor's Wedding

Ivor and Sheila with Ivor's Daughter Deborah

Ivor's Parents, James and Florence (dec'd)

Jane and John's Wedding

Roof during repairs

A satisfied Ivor on completion

Our new pond and patio

Proud Grandparents, Ivor and Sheila, with baby Julia

Sheila "swinging the lead"

Feeding time for the cats!

Doting Sheila with Freddie

Ivor, Laura, John, Julia and Jane

Ivor enjoying time out with his Grandchildren, Julia and Laura

Eve, our Medium, with cats Cindy and Tibby

Entrance to Millcroft Bungalow

Sadly our last Family group taken at Millcroft Bungalow

Ivor and Sheila's handiwork – conservatory and garden

Jane with Julia and Laura

Laura and Julia at their Graduations

Rows of Chrysanthemums

Boxes of beautiful blooms

*Laura, Dave and little Jack, Sheila and Ivor's Great Grandson
(and he is!)*

Sheila, Sue, John and Dave (their son) on holiday in Tenerife

Jane and Paul (Daughter and Son-in-Law)

Mike and Dad having a laugh at one of the wedding do's

Brother John and the lucky Husbands of all we girls!!

Ivor was enlisted to prepare the seating arrangements on the large patio surrounding one side of the bungalow. John, together with Mike (when available) offered to help. First of all, they gathered together all the oil drums they could find – there were plenty on site – and then found as many long planks of wood that were available to provide the seating which was to be long benches in an 'L' shape along the wall surrounding the patio. (Ivor had bought in some second-hand timber ready to be used for outside building purposes.) I then set to work to find as many old curtains, 'throws' and cushions for the planking – we didn't want splinters causing any problems! (Mini-skirts were in fashion at that time!) Ivor then constructed some tables (using more oil drums and wider planks, and I then found plenty of sheets to act as tablecloths. We also borrowed some extra chairs and trestle tables from our little Dawlish Christian Spiritualist Church.

In case of rain, Ivor also rigged up some plastic sheeting (some old tunnelling from a job lot he had bought) and anchored it down with some fertiliser bags (ready for our future horticultural enterprises) placed at strategic points on our accommodating flat roof.

Ivor was also in charge of providing the music but he drew the line at being the DJ. He rigged up a speaker outside and I borrowed as many CDs from the family as I could – we had quite an assortment! Lonny Donegan, Neil Diamond, The Beatles, etc etc!!! Someone even loaned us a Gracie Fields, (I think they were joking!) but we were never having 'Murphy and the Bricks'!

On the day of the wedding, the sun shone brightly from early morning to late at night. Everything went splendidly except for the hundred or so individual jellies that I had placed on the tables outside which all promptly melted in the sun. Not to worry, we managed to place them all in the freezer and they were ready at the appointed time to give to our hungry guests, together with the sumptuous spread all provided by the 'Melmoth Family's Deluxe Catering Corps' as well as the trifles, sausage rolls, vol-au-vents, not forgetting our family's speciality: 'egg sandwiches'. I made the wedding cake and Margaret iced it. She was an expert at anything to do with cooking, and excelled herself – the cake was fit for a Queen (and King!)

This was to be the pattern for future celebrations, whether it was a birthday, christening, whatever, for any member of the Melmoth 'clan'. We always made a point of having a photograph taken of the eight of us on every occasion but, when our dear Margaret was the first to pass, that was the end of our 'family group' on film at any rate!

The wedding went without a hitch – a lovely occasion – but now it was time to set about putting the garden to right. Our first purchase was a giant barrow from one of the agricultural merchants to tow behind an old ride-on mower that we had inherited from the previous occupier.

As with the other two ride-ons that we were to purchase in the future, Ivor made a metal chute and placed it in such a way that it blew all the grass cuttings from the mower into a trailer with a wire mesh roof and sides, to catch it. This dispensed with having to keep emptying the box, especially if he was mowing the field!

First of all we had to cut our way into the front entrance which was very overgrown, mostly with brambles (the bungalow had been empty for some time). We then grassed the small strip of land adjoining the hedge outside our gates, placed some curbing around it and finally threaded white chain through some oak posts. It actually looked very smart!

Ivor eventually bought a chain saw (although he never used it when climbing and cutting down trees etc.). This is not my favourite tool but he made sure that he followed all the safety rules to the letter and was always very careful when using it. In a few weeks, we had tidied the entrance and most of the garden, and I always laughed my head off to see Ivor disappearing down the field, with the barrow piled high, like a mobile bonfire, and was always surprised to see him reach the bottom of the field with most of the load still intact. We had then to light a bonfire (our favourite job). How we loved it as we were far enough away from any houses for the smoke to be a nuisance. Happy days!

Besides the brambles we also had to cut down one or two of the trees that had become dangerously tall, with large branches falling off and causing a hazard, so Ivor used to climb almost to the top with our tallest ladder, and cut it down, bit by bit, using his hand saw. We hated to see it go but when one branch narrowly missed Ivor when he was cutting the lawn that was its death knell – it had to go. I was always there to help on the end of a rope, if it was necessary, to keep the branch in check and guide it to the ground, away from the other shrubs, but most times I was told to keep out of the way, but I became indispensable when the time came to load the barrow and get rid of the remains of our poor tree strewn all over the lawn. Ivor then had some very large logs to cut up with the chain saw and plenty of pieces of fir to get our bonfires crackling. The logs (kept in the barn) also came in very handy for our log fire which was installed in our dining room a few years later which Ivor loved to light and 'feed' to his heart's content.

We then purchased a second-hand concrete mixer, together with all the materials necessary to extend the open hay shed, using concrete blocks and extending the roof, making a very useful barn for all the machinery we were starting to accumulate. Ivor tried his hand at plastering the concrete blocks and made a good job of it. He also concreted the yard in front of the barn, and the two existing stables, and used railway sleepers to make sturdy doors for them, providing excellent work sheds, secure with locks and bolts.

It was good to get the barn completed as, whilst it was open to all winds and weather; we had quite a few stray cats making their homes inside it. In the end we had ten – and eventually some kittens to go with them, and although they cost us a fortune in cat food, they soon made short work of the vermin that were quite prolific at that time. Ivor later put a cat flap in the barn to allow them to come and go at their leisure as by now he had made them ten wooden compartments, sited on one of the walls, with bits of blanket in each one – their own padded cells!

I took some of the cats down to the vet to be 'doctored'. That soon put an end to the kitten situation although one cat did manage to escape my clutches and presented me with three beautiful kittens. I fell in love with all of them (these were in addition to the existing ten – they all had names) but Ivor said enough was enough and that they had to go and so, with a sad heart, I took them to a cat shelter and left them behind, breaking my heart all the way home only to receive a call from the shelter after three days begging me to come and take them back because they were causing an uproar at being separated, and, as a result, was making too much noise for the rest of the residents. Of course, we had to bring them back and, although I did try very hard to find them homes (honestly!) we kept them in the end, and even Ivor fell in love with them, especially Tabitha, the tabby one. My favourites were Tom (the black one) and Rupert (the Persian-like grey) and, although, eating with the rest of the strays in the barn, they often came in and spent the evenings with us, much to my delight.

How I loved those cats – they all mostly died of old age and are all buried in the garden.

Now that is not quite the end of the story regarding cats by any means. About 2012 (after all our cats had long since ascended to the big cat shelter in the sky) we started to be visited by a cat, a beautiful big grey with white markings, very friendly, that came into the garden. I fell in love with him, called him Tiger, and wanted to feed him but knew that this was wrong because he obviously belonged to someone; he was in such wonderful condition. One day, I was talking to our next-door neighbour who lived on the farm and asked about the cat and who he belonged to. She said that his owner (an employee on the farm) had died a month or so ago and that she was feeding him now, but that they had a cat and some dogs on the farm and that it was not a very satisfactory arrangement. By this time another of my neighbours (a dear friend who had a cat of her own) also informed me of Freddie's predicament so in the end I offered to feed him and he came to live with us – well, sort of.

His real name is Freddie and he is very much his own cat, very independent and when we first took him under our wing he wouldn't stay indoors unless the door was left open, in case he needed to make a quick getaway, I presume. Well, in the end Ivor lost patience, and got fed up with having to reach for his coat (so he pretended) whenever Freddie graced us with his presence and said that if I wanted to keep him I had to teach him how to close the b***** door, and in the end Freddie eventually came to trust us and allowed us to close the door, well sometimes, but as I am now on my own, I keep it open until he is settled and fast asleep and doesn't care about the b***** door being shut any more. What we do for our animals! Now that we are in another lockdown he is coming indoors much more, and I believe and hope, he is mellowing in his old age! I love him to bits but have to be very careful when he rolls onto his back to play as he likes his tummy tickled, and I need a strong pair of gloves to keep his claws at bay. He also likes to dig my carpet and takes great offence at me shouting at him and will sulk for hours, turning his back on me, but it is surprising what a dish of Whiskas will do to put him in the right mood once again!

As well as preparing the land for the cider apples and chrysanthemums, we were also trying to put the bungalow in order – especially the flat roof. Ivor had spent days in our little office with his set square and graph paper and eventually emerged to show me that he had made a plan to repair the roof. I said yes, how was he going to patch it up? I knew that it was leaking in a corner of the dining room. My mouth dropped open when he said, 'No, we have to repair all of it, all 12,000 sq. metres of it.' Well, I didn't like the sound of having to repair the whole roof but he said, 'Don't worry, it shouldn't take too long.' 'Much' I thought but he was determined to do the job so I went along with it, helping him to draw up a list of materials that would be needed. He then rang this and that firm to get the right prices and, in the end the day came when we were all ready and waiting for the 'off'.

I gazed at the pile of roofing felt. 'How on earth are we going to get that onto the roof?' I asked, 'With this?' he said, pointing to a contraption that I had seen him working on before. 'It is a hoist and it will save us hours of work as well as backache. But now we have to take off the gravel and the old roofing felt as well.' He then proceeded to climb up the ladder and asked me to hand up a rake, broom and his box of tools. I asked him what he wanted me to do and he said, 'Make a cup of tea when I shout.' After a couple of hours the shout came and I stood at the bottom of the ladder and then he descended, asking where his tea was?

After the break I returned to the bottom of the ladder but first was instructed to pass up some empty buckets that he had put to one side, by attaching each of them to the metal hook linked to the hoist fixed to the roof. He then turned the handle on the hoist and promptly lifted them up. He said he would shout when he was ready to lower the full buckets. I thought 'here we go. This is going to be a job and no mistake!' but when the first bucket was lowered, all I had to do was empty it carefully whilst it was still on the rope – let the gravel fall in a neat pile, then allow the empty bucket to be lifted up by the hoist once again. Wonderful for me but he was having to rake up all the gravel and fill the buckets with a spade. What a job – but he was in his element. He eventually finished gathering it all up, and there it was, in a neat pile on the ground, ready for the next stage. I put the kettle on!

Now he had to get the roll of roofing felt on to the roof. How? By turning the handle and pulling it inches at a time by the hoist, and with me being told to stand back out of the way – which I did willingly!

Next, there were five-gallon drums of what I can only describe as tar-like thick substance to haul up on to the roof, to stick down the roofing felt. How did he get the drums on to the roof? By ropes tied around their middle and rolled up on two ladders, with him hauling them up one by one by turning the handle and me guiding each one with a long wooden batten to keep it straight on the ladders. I was to stand to the side in case one of them slipped – I'm glad to say none of them did! I foolishly made a joke about hoping that the stoppers were safely plugged in – then I noticed Ivor's face – he wasn't laughing!

After safely getting these drums onto the roof I saw Ivor pouring this tar-like substance into a bucket and brushing it onto the roof, small areas at a time. I climbed the ladder (it was anchored firmly in the grass) and watched from the top rung. He had his Stanley knife with him, cutting and smoothing the roofing felt as he went. I asked very helpfully if there was any way I could help. 'Yes please', he said, 'Make a cup of tea!'

I am not sure how many days it took him – or how many cups of tea – but every night we looked at the weather forecast and every night it was bad news – but fortunately the rain didn't materialise. Overcast threatening clouds – but no rain. Our gods were certainly looking after us. Even to this day I cannot believe that it remained dry, but dry it was.

At last we reached the final stage. The empty buckets came out and now it was just a simple matter – of filling them and putting them on the hook, and simple it was. Ivor lined up the buckets and we did it together, with Ivor placing each one under the hoist. All I had to do was place the hook on the handles and he pulled them up, one by one, and we started spreading, raking the gravel into the corners and making sure that all the felt was covered.

What a job. It had been a lot of work for Ivor, and a lot of nail-biting for me, but he said he felt good, he had achieved his aim, and thank goodness he had no after effects – no aching back, shoulders or limbs – and, best of all, the roof didn't leak anymore!

Well, we ploughed on. I suppose we were afraid that if we stopped we would never start again! The next big job was the oil tank which had started to leak – another urgent job! First of all, Ivor ordered a large 1000 litre tank from an ironmonger (I presume) and then borrowed some oil drums from one of our domestic oil suppliers to empty the tank.

Next, he borrowed some scaffolding poles from a builder friend he knew. Luckily, we had a very convenient garden wall outside the tank house door, exactly the same height as the base on which our old tank was sited, so it was just a matter of positioning the poles from the base of the tank to the wall. He then used a broom handle and levered the tank on to the poles, sliding it on to the wall and eventually onto the garden.

The next job was to place the new tank onto the poles in the garden and gradually ease it back into the tank house. He poured all the oil from the drums back into the tank which was once again in place and ready to be used. Simple once again – as Ivor had said.

In between working to prepare the soil for our major crop – the chrysanthemums – and installing plastic tunnels etc. we started again on the garden. We had removed a small fish pond in the middle of the lawn, which had previously been badly sited, and had made the lawn very uneven. Ivor then made a plan (all on graph paper) to site a large concrete fish pond next door to a second patio, and ordered all the paving slabs, decorative stone walling, sand, cement and gravel that was needed.

The concrete mixer was again brought into action and then it was necessary for me to use my muscles (which I didn't mind in the least) to fill the various buckets to keep feeding it. We set to work with a will – I couldn't wait for the pond to be completed and the patio to be laid – our first granddaughter was shortly to arrive and I wanted it completed for her christening – and it was. We made a big celebration of filling the pond (no leaks) to mark the occasion. We also gave it the right treatment to make sure it was safe for the fish to reside in and once again had a day out with John and Sue to buy some lovely gold, silver and black ones).

Ivor had found a lead pump to place it at the head of the pond, and installed electricity to make the pool light up, the waterfall from the pump to cascade into the pond and a lovely fountain (bought second-hand) to do its job perfectly. The patio was then laid and hey presto, it was all ready for the big day and we have photographs to show us all sat on the wall of the pond, together with the proud parents, (not to mention the proud grandparents) enjoying some G&Ts!

I might add that although the pond is still functioning – Ivor put a filter system in later on – the fountain still works but sad to say a heron took a fancy to all our lovely fish and scoffed the lot. I did have a cry – I used to feed the fish religiously in the summer and loved to see them come up every mealtime – so now we have a net placed over the pond, purchased from our local merchants, and there is now no danger of the fish ever being gobbled up again in the future – and to think I used to like herons!

After the patio was laid we set to work on the lawn around the bungalow. We scrapped some beds and created more new convenient ones, pruning and cutting for days on end, with the compost heap getting higher and higher, and the bonfires almost raging out of control sometimes, but with me standing nearby with a hosepipe just in case! We had to be careful in the summer, but thank goodness we never had to use it!

We levelled the earth, sowing a lot of grass seed – sacks of it – and then we (no, Ivor) rolled it in with a big roller we hired. We also pruned a lot of the shrubs and trees but it was a beautiful garden even then, with masses of camelias, rhododendrons, azaleas, cherry trees and a super magnolia tree – it has always been at its best in the spring as most gardens are!

Apart from the flowering trees, we created a small orchard which we have to this day, although now a little depleted. Once again John and Sue came with us to buy the fruit trees – at one time we even elicited Percy Thrower's help (one of the big-name gardening experts) in one of the nurseries he was visiting on that particular day. He was a lovely man and gave us a lot of advice. We settled for Victoria plums (2) conference and William pears (1 each) coxes apples (2) Blenheim Orange Apples (2) and 2 Bramleys (and of course, approx. 500 (I think) cider apple trees but not from that nursery and not for the small orchard)!! We also bought some raspberry canes (summer and autumn) and they thrived, especially when being grown a few yards from the septic tank! They were never so good once they were sited elsewhere!

Whilst we were planting some strawberries in quite a big patch of ground we were visited by a man (he came to be a very dear friend to us) and said he would like to tend the strawberry patch for us as a trial, and if we were happy with his work, would we employ him? Well, he excelled himself and produced a crop of the largest strawberries (and raspberries for that matter) that we had ever seen so we didn't hesitate to hire him, and he went on to be the first of many expert part-time gardeners that we had the good luck to hire. One of them – Richard – was the head gardener of a big estate before he retired) and all were worth their weight in gold, and served us sequentially and steadfastly for many, many years.

Stan would sit outside his shed in his deck chair, on his breaks, and toast us with his flask, regaling us with lovely stories of his life in Dawlish and making us laugh our heads off, he was so funny (I can see him now!) He was especially involved with amateur dramatics – pantomimes in particular – and I remember him saying once 'Sheila and Ivor, thank you for this – waving his arms in front of him – this time of wine and roses.' He was a wonderful, happy man.

Now, we have a lady gardener (Jenny) – an absolute gem – and will do anything that is needed. She will take on any heavy building work: laying concrete slabs, repairing barn roofs, etc, etc. down to weeding the flower beds on her hands and knees! What would I do without her?

Between whiles we concentrated on the conditions of the agricultural tie, and once again had a lovely day out (when the time was right) with John and Sue to visit a grower, I think in Essex, to purchase some chrysanths – rootstock – settling for the big bloom varieties, together with some colourful sprays, and some very good advice. John had been growing chrysanths as a hobby for many years so was able to give us a lot of expert advice himself and also, a lot of help and support together with dear Sue. They helped us most weekends (they were both working full-time themselves).

In the meantime, we had bought two large second-hand plastic tunnels and Ivor made large trays out of some galvanised sheeting – he had previously worked as a sheet metal worker in his father's workshop from the age of 15 onwards, but had to stop when he caught TB at an early age of 19 years.

I must just tell you what Ivor told me of his life in his father's workshop. He said he had to ensure that the furnace was always up to temperature when needed and that he often used to have to go and fetch large metal sheets strapped to his bike, resting on the pedals (this at 15 years old) from merchants at the top of Exeter – their workshop was at the bottom! – until his father bought a small Austin 7. He then had to put the sheets on the roof – he probably managed the sheeting better on his bike! He also said he had to go to London once with his father to get some materials they needed for a certain job (they made all sorts of utensils for beekeeping etc. and for domestic items) and he said he will never forget the look on his father's face, when they were in the middle of London (in their little Austin 7) with traffic coming at them from left, right and centre – a great big double-decker bus dwarfing them on one side and a great big transporter on the other – and saying 'Now I know what a sardine feels like!'

To get back to the tunnels – unfortunately we chose the wrong day to try to put them up. Sue was holding one end when all at once a gust of wind sent her flying – she is very tiny – but we all held on to her and managed to bring her back to earth, literally speaking!

Now, we were ready to set out the field for planting. Together with the many rolls of square mesh wire netting, Ivor had bought a number of wooden stakes from a timber merchant (he had worked out the quantities he would need beforehand) then ploughed the field with a small cultivator that he had picked up quite cheaply in a small garden machinery shop on the outskirts of Torquay. I had to scatter the fertiliser, as he said, in equal quantities – of course I did – when I remembered not to go over a section twice! We then started to mark out the rows, inserting two wooden stakes at the top and bottom of the rows and some in the middle for support. The wire-netting was then unwound and fixed to the stakes. Now, we transplanted the roots that we grew in the trays of soil in the tunnels to the rows of wires in the field, and they eventually grew into beautiful plants (tall and straight within the wires) which needed disbudding every evening when we arrived home from work, approx. two hours each time. We were thrilled with the blooms – we couldn't believe that we – amateurs (although John wasn't an amateur!) had produced such wonderful specimens. Ivor had already made enquiries from a firm of wholesalers and agreed a price for each bloom so at the weekends we cut them and placed them in buckets overnight and then boxed them early in the mornings in big flat-packed cardboard boxes, purchased from the wholesaler, which had to be put together before use.

This was the pattern of our lives for the next seven or eight years or so. Every season we salvaged the roots, washed them and stored them away until they were required the next year. We usually started at Easter. At intervals we purchased some new rootstock, to keep the standard up, allowing some of the old blooms to develop into sprays. They were much sought after as well as the giant blooms. It all worked like a dream (thanks to John and Sue in the beginning) and we used the stakes and netting year after year, but whatever we received for the blooms was ploughed back, and more, into the sprays, fertiliser etc. that was needed for the next season, and also to pay for the rootstock and cider apple trees that we purchased in the beginning. We never broke even and thank heavens for our salaries to pay for the mortgage, but we loved our life at Millcroft, despite having to earn it!

After about four years into our routine (1984), I had fibroids and needed a hysterectomy. Ivor arranged for a doctor's appointment in Harley Street under the ministry's private medical insurance scheme that we paid into and an operation was carried out at Benendon Hospital in Kent. We went by car and Ivor took a week off work and came with me when I had my operation. (He also treated himself to an hour's flying lesson and was proud to tell me that he flew above the hospital at one time and waved to me lying, unknowingly, down below!) He had always wanted to fly and had taken several flying lessons when he could afford them. He was called up for his national service – he had requested, before his illness, that he wanted to join the RAF, but of course, after his medical, was declared unfit for duty. This has always been a thorn in his side!

All went well with the operation and I returned to the office after three months and was given 'light duties' – the job of secretary to a panel of three experts. The panel had to consider appeals from farmers and I had to write a letter accepting or declining their appeals, and if accepting, calculating the amount that would be granted in the letter – quite a job to get it done within three months with the amount of appeals that had to be heard!

Computers were only just coming into fashion at that time but Ivor insisted on writing a programme on our little home computer to try to help me. I refused his help at first but when he proved what a godsend it would be, I quickly changed my mind. There were very long calculations involved, to five decimal places, but with his programme, all I had to do was enter all the various figures involved, and then (without having to wrack my brain to do the long calculation on my old-fashioned calculator) up came the amount of quota to be granted. I couldn't believe my luck. Head office thought I was a genius as I was the only one over all the country that was getting every letter right. Unfortunately, our office was due to be modernised and 30 monitors had to be set up to a main-frame, and because I had done so well as secretary to the panel – I received praise but no remuneration – I had been chosen to be in charge, and although I argued that it had been Ivor who had been the expert, and that I didn't have a clue about computers, I was given the job and had to train at Southampton and London over a three-week period. Luckily, a young computer expert was drafted in to deputise for me to carry out this quite onerous task (he was great) and looking back on it now, I realise that I enjoyed the experience very much. I also realise, in coming to grips with the mainframe and all its complexities, it gave me great satisfaction.

Back to our gardening enterprise, John and Sue helped us most weekends and when we had got ourselves established, after a couple of years John, Sue, David (their ten-year-old son), Ivor and I went to Tenerife for a lovely holiday, and we continued having super holidays with them most years after that all our lives, but not always with Dave. (As most teenagers, he preferred to go holidaying with his friends instead.)

Once we had got the growing of the chrysanths up and running Ivor ordered the cider apple trees – hundreds of them, or so it seemed to me. We then purchased some more netting, small mesh this time, to put around every tree root to discourage the rabbits, but this was a losing game. As fast as we put them in, the rabbits pulled them out the next day. (It didn't help that the five acres were two fields away from us either – unfortunately the field we should have purchased was changed at the last minute.) We gave up after a few years!

Ivor said he would finish off the rabbits with his gun (he had previously been an Olympic coach at his local rifle club) but he never did. Once we started our spiritual work, come to think of it, he never used his gun again!

Apart from our physical work we were now regularly attending the Dawlish Christian Spiritualist Church and were developing our healing skills, attending courses on Dartmoor organised by our dear friend Ron, (the area secretary of the National Federation of Spiritual Healers) and we were invited to join their development group, meeting every week on Dartmoor and in our home the next.

We continued to work the land attached to the bungalow at the weekends, and any other time available, but mostly disbudding every evening after work, but we kept at it until we both retired in 1992 – after two lovely office retirement parties and saying goodbye to all our friends and colleagues. We were both sad to go as we had both enjoyed our jobs and the lovely friends we had made and then had to leave behind.

Once we retired we gave up growing the chrysanths – quite glad to stop actually in the end (I wonder why) but now we started to grow some lovely vegetables in their place, and it was about this time that our spiritual work really took off.

We were asked by spirit (through our Medium) if we would tour the country channelling talks to other groups. After two years, meeting some really lovely people, we settled down to continue with our healing work, but were also able to concentrate on the bungalow, and our two lovely granddaughters, who were then 9 and 11 years old respectively, taking them to The Miniature Pony Centre, Woodland Park and all the other attractions and adventure playgrounds for children. We also took them riding and sometimes skating and swimming – lovely days out. They also used to stay with us for school holidays. We were in our element, and they always came down to us for Christmas – Ivor ringing the bells as my father did when I was a child on Christmas Eve, heralding Father Xmas' imminent arrival – causing them to scream and race quickly into bed, leaving us to enjoy the Sherry and mince pies left lovingly for him.

Once we retired we joined the Christian Spiritualist Church's Healing Team on Tuesday afternoons, and continued to hold spiritual meetings at our home.

In our spare time we were now ready to concentrate on updating the bungalow, with some money now available from our 'lump' sums, and burning a hole in our pockets, I don't think! We knew exactly how it was going to be spent, with amounts allotted for each project.

Once the new window was installed in the kitchen we decided that the kitchen itself needed attention – we had lived in it for the last 13 years so considered that it was time to make the changes – and asked for an estimate from one of the big firms, but Ivor decided that the cost was far too high and said he could do it for half the price, and then set out to prove that he could!

Once again he made a plan before we went to a big store – I think it was Texas – and ordered the fittings. We both decided on the timber style we would like and ordered it, all flat-packed. I think it was in Rosewood, with the dining room side in Mahogany.

The big day arrived. It was sunny outside I remember when it was delivered, and off we went – unpacking it all very methodically, laying it all out on the patio. Everything was laid out, together with the screws, handles etc. for each cupboard. Ivor had bought a new electric drill and in no time it was fitted. We then bought some lovely tiles we both fell in love with – little scenes of deer in leafy glades, old-fashioned but our style I am afraid – and the kitchen was eventually finished, with my dear nephew Nigel (who is in the trade) cutting the kitchen tops to size and making a superb job of them. I remember looking at it, not believing that this beautiful kitchen was actually ours. It was then finished off with some matching linoleum and then it was perfect. To cap it all Ivor did manage to create the kitchen for half the price quoted!

We then ordered the windows for the rest of the bungalow and once they were installed we visited a local remnant shop and decided on the curtains – long velvet ones with linings for the lounge and dining room, and matching curtains and bedspreads for the bedrooms (seconds I might add for the bedrooms – the patterns were a little askew but were hardly noticeable. The material was all laid out on the lounge floor and expertly cut, with me pinning when required – but most times watching on the sidelines – Ivor could do it so much quicker himself, and was quite happy to do so! This was a mammoth job and the new sewing machine we had just purchased was red-hot by the time he finished! (It was no surprise that Ivor was able to make the curtains – he had surprised me earlier in our married life when he had made a skirt for me because I had not seen one I liked in the shops, and had even made an evening dress for me also!)

After the curtains were made we set to work to find suitable wallpaper and ceiling paper and proceeded to decorate, but first of all we had to dispense with an archway between the lounge and dining room, and Ivor replaced it with some lovely glass oak doors, which made the lounge and dining rooms so much warmer.

After this we decided that we would like a conservatory and once we had decided which side of the bungalow it was to be sited on we went to the nearest garden nursery and chose a metal framed one in a sale. Ivor then got the concrete mixer out once again and built a platform for the base, and made some steps leading to it. Once it was finished he cut all the hedges down to half-size in the garden to give us a better outlook. We never realised what a wonderful view we had until it was revealed!

We then had a go at the bathroom, Ivor taking away a wall separating the toilet to make it much bigger. (We already had a cloakroom so didn't need a separate toilet.) We then visited the Tile Shop and picked the tiles, which were cemented on to the walls from floor to ceiling. I loved it when it was finished.

We have since had our bathroom beautifully modernised by a dear friend of ours who also updated the glass in the porch and hall and internal doors. Since Ivor passed I had slipped on the kitchen floor and had fallen, breaking the glass in the door with my arm. Luckily I only sustained a few cuts and bruises but there and then decided that the old original glass all had to be replaced by toughened glass – once again our friend Terry did a very professional job!

The last decorating we did was to our bedroom. In our latter years, instead of going on cruises we used to have our summer holidays in a lovely hotel in Cornwall. We very much admired the decor of the last room we occupied – it was sunny and bright, the curtains having large flowers on a yellow background. When we arrived home the next day Ivor said, 'Let's see if we can get some material like the curtains we admired in our hotel room', so off we trotted to our favourite material shop to find a similar pattern. Once again Ivor set about cutting and pinning, producing the curtains, bedspread and even a lampshade of the same material. He then made a very professional pelmet for the window together with a super headboard. Great!

When he was in his 76th year he decided that he wanted to take up Turning – he loved wood of every shape and size which stemmed from an early age, when he attended evening woodworking classes at the Exeter Technical College, at 15 years old, and made a beautiful Oak sewing box for his mother, also a lovely oak bureau, and an expanding dining room table, that I possess to this day.

As he now had an itch for trying his hand at something new, we had another day out to find a suitable lathe and eventually found the right one with everything he required.

He then set about enlarging his workshop, once again putting the concrete mixer to good use and me helping with the buckets, etc. etc. He also replaced some roofing sheets that let the daylight in, and two small windows for his workshop. He then looked on the internet for suitable courses he could take to learn the art, and settled on one in Totnes that he thought suited his purpose, and it did. The tutor was excellent and he thoroughly enjoyed the course, and met some really nice people in the process. The family and I are now the proud owners of some beautiful wooden bowls of all shapes, and sizes, and various other items that he took great pleasure in producing.

Ivor had always known that he had the 'gift' of healing but had not known how to develop it until he was speaking to a friend, a very good Medium, who told him to go to his nearest spiritualist church. He made enquiries and eventually attended his first healing session at the Dawlish Christian Spiritualist Church, and from thereon, never looked back. After a time he persuaded me to go with him, telling me that the healing group were lovely people who voluntarily attended the church every week solely to give love and healing to the people who came before them. He had been taught by this group, (who had recognised that he was a natural healer) on how to connect to our Creator and to be able to channel energy to help the person sitting in front of him, and on his first healing was able to help a man with a frozen shoulder who was so delighted that he shouted 'Its free, its free', waving his arm excitedly in the air to the consternation of everyone present. Of course, this was all the incentive that Ivor needed, and he never looked back, helping many people with their ailments over the years.

We did contact our local surgery once to offer our services – i.e. the doctors would first give their services and then we would follow afterwards with our spiritual healing to help with the curing of the ailment. Unfortunately, the doctor Ivor spoke to didn't even listen to what he had to offer and just said, 'Oh don't, the thought makes the hairs on my neck stand on end!' This was not the reaction of other surgeries we know of who jumped at the chance and employed healers with great results!

Writing about this I now realise just how wonderful Ivor's healing really was. In 2002, my doctor was suspicious of the pain I was getting in my left side when I attended the surgery. He gave me a test to carry out which eventually led to a cancer operation of the bowel which was caught very early. Ivor gave me healing after the operation, guided by spirit – it was like lightning, zig-zagging into my body, incredible energy – and, together, with the foresight of my doctor and the surgeon's wonderful skill, I was completely cured, with no added chemo or radio treatment.

I convalesced in Brighton for a week (Jane and the family paid me a wonderful welcome visit) and when we returned home Ivor arranged a holiday to Tenerife. After this we continued with our 'home refurbishments', and enjoying life with our grandchildren as before. We also treated ourselves to lovely cruises with Sue and John every year.

In June, 2008, disaster struck when Ivor had a heart attack and was rushed into hospital, necessitating some stents being fitted. He made a remarkable recovery but not quite in time to attend the inaugural meeting of our new healer group held at the Dawlish Christian Spiritualist Church.

We had decided to take up BAHA's (British Alliance of Healing Associations) offer to set up our own healing group, under their umbrella, and so the South West Association of Spiritual Healers was born. We never looked back, using the church as our venue as before.

After the Inaugural meeting (we had seventy odd members), we went from strength to strength and attended many festivals of light etc. with some of our healers and students, and Ivor and I also attended various halls and other venues (once we were kindly invited to speak at a local pub) giving talks on healing, soul rescue and other spiritual matters.

In 2013, I started to suffer from diverticulitis (which my surgeon warned me might be a problem when he gave me the all clear for the bowel cancer I suffered in 2002. It was a problem and caused a leakage into my bladder and I took a turn for the worst and spent four days in the Intensive Care Unit of the R.D & E Hospital in Exeter, having succumbed to Peritonitis and Septicaemia. Once again Ivor gave me healing after the operation which helped to save my life, together with the wonderful work of the surgeon. Unfortunately, this necessitated a stoma being fitted which, when I got used to it – by mainly eating the right food and not too much of it – I can honestly say I have been able to manage very well. I can certainly recommend it to anyone suffering from serious stomach problems, but all this happened to me when I was 80 years old – I would probably feel very differently if it had happened to me in my twenties – but when it is life or death…I digress. Going back to healing, I remember especially once when I am afraid I did not show myself in a very good light at all! It was during a meal at a Red Cross anniversary dinner we were invited to by a dear friend, when a door was flung open and an elderly lady, who was suddenly taken ill, was placed on a chair on a small balcony to give her some air. Her son and his wife, who were both doctors, immediately rushed to her aid as did, to my horror, Ivor saying, 'I have to go to her.' Well, being the coward that I was, I stayed cemented to my chair whilst he, unabashed, rushed to the balcony, together with several of her other relatives, all doctors I might add. I saw him kneel down at her side and catch hold of her hand (I was expecting to see him thrown off the balcony at any moment) but wonder of wonders I saw her grab at his hand and place it on her forehead, ignoring her concerned relatives nearby. She told Ivor (he informed me afterwards) that she had suffered a blinding headache and had lost her sight, but that as soon as his hand touched her forehead she had felt warmth and a wonderful peace, and knew that she was going to be alright. After a few minutes she put his hand to her lips and kissed it, saying she felt much better, the headache had gone and that her sight had been restored with no ill effects at all. She went on to enjoy the evening and when she left, on her way out she made a point of thanking Ivor for his wonderful healing.

We were flying high on our journey home (the doctors didn't know everything!) and at the next meeting we had with our Medium, our spirit friends congratulated Ivor on his bravery in sticking his neck out, as he had done, to offer his help, which had worked spectacularly. The lady had fully recovered and, much to my relief, thankfully there was not a mention of me failing in my duty!

After this we had some other healings that will always remain in my memory, one being the time when a friend of

Ivor's asked him if we would give his wife some healing. She suffered from arthritis and was confined to a wheelchair. We made an appointment to visit (going quite a long way actually) but when we arrived she point-blank refused to see us saying that she didn't want any healing, especially not from a man. We said that was okay, if she didn't want healing she didn't want healing, and so prepared to leave when she changed her mind and said that perhaps it would be okay if I gave her the healing and not Ivor. We agreed but as we always worked together I stood behind her and Ivor stood to the side, quietly directing the energy where it was needed, but we could tell from the beginning that she had put up a block and there was no way she could receive the energy. Her husband stood on the other side. When we finished we asked the lady if she had felt anything. 'Nothing', she said, 'Nothing at all', but all at once her dear husband said, 'Look, look, I can use it', waving his arm above his head. Strangely enough this was another frozen shoulder – he had had this complaint for some years and Ivor, because he knew of the block she had used, directed the healing to his friend instead who was very thrilled and was completely cured as we discovered afterwards. How we laughed all the way home.

Another time we were asked by my sister Gladys if we would give healing to her dear friend Mary who had cancer. We visited and could see that she was very ill. She was in bed and we both went to her to hold her hands and to give her words of love and encouragement. She was obviously in great pain, and we started to give her the healing which we could feel was very strong. Ivor looked out the window whilst he was doing so (he told me this afterwards) and said that all at once dear Mary's spirit was there beside him, looking out the window as well, but seeing an entirely different scene to what he was seeing, i.e. obviously one in heaven and said, 'Oh look, Ivor, isn't it marvellous, all these beautiful colours.' After we finished (it was not very long before she died) we realised that although Mary was suffering great pain in the physical, she was at peace and out of pain in the spiritual. That was a big lesson for us and our Master (through our Medium Eve) explained that this was the pattern; the spirit was taken before the body actually died.

It was not many days after this that we came across our one and only accident that we have ever experienced together. As we turned a corner we saw a motor-cyclist in the road, and just across from him a car that had skidded, presumably to avoid him. Ivor quickly pulled to the side of the road. He then took out the two car rugs that we kept in the car and told me to try to cover the motor-cyclist with one and the other under his head whilst asking the car driver to ring for the police and ambulance. (Unbeknown to anybody we both directed healing energy to the motor-cyclist). Ivor then went to direct the traffic. In no time the Police and ambulance arrived and took over. How pleased I was that I had not been on my own – Ivor had kept a cool head and a clear mind and had known exactly what to do and how to do it. Good job he did, I wouldn't have had a clue!

Rewind to our spiritual mode. Once I realised that the Dawlish Christian Spiritualist Church was there to give love and comfort and was not the weird place that I had been led to believe, I quickly became an addict, wanting to know more, and I did!

Whilst becoming spiritual healers we have also been engaged in other spiritual work at home, mainly bringing light and love to the world and carrying out soul rescue with many mediums, and receiving channelling from wonderful masters, and up to Ivor's death on September 14, 2015, continuing Soul Rescue, every week, with Ivor organising each session.

Having been a spiritualist for the last forty years or so I have met a number of mediums, indeed many are my closest friends, who have loved ones who have passed (died) that have returned to be with them (and this is nothing unusual to us) so when Ivor came back to be with me after his passing and helped me, as he always did when on the earth plane, I was thrilled as I missed his physical presence so much.

Of course, he has many duties he has to fulfil spiritually and said that he would not always be available, and he isn't always as he is a master in his own right, but I can always contact him in an emergency. We communicate through my pendant and now I can rely on him as I always could, and I know he keeps me safe, night and day. He is always there when I need to speak to him, and of course I am never lonely.

When Ivor asked me if I would continue with the soul rescue service to help all the dear ones who are now passing in such great numbers (our medium was not able to do this physically because of the rules governing the pandemic) I jumped at the chance and now we sit and perform this service twice a week (it was much more in the early days). I would add that Ivor, in his light body, is exactly the same now as he was on the earth plane – he wears a suit with white shirt and tie when he comes to the people we rescue – he would never be able to get near them if he appeared wearing a robe.

There are thousands and thousands of Soul Rescue groups like ours, and they are necessary because unfortunately many people in our world today have not sought to find out about life after death, do not believe in God and Jesus, and indeed, in a lot of cases – using their freewill – which God has granted to all of us, do not wish to know either, and will not seek any spiritual knowledge because they consider it not right to do so (or for many other numerous reasons), although Jesus told us to 'seek and ye shall find', therefore, when these people die they do not follow the light and so they miss their chance to go forward into their new lives, and are left in limbo (sometimes in ghost form and frighten people when they see them, whereas, all the 'ghosts' need is help). Most people of course believe in God and Jesus and know about life after death, and follow the light and go forward, as our dear mother and father did, and then of course they have no problem in accessing their new lives.

Our friends in spirit have said they need people like us to carry out soul rescues to show the ones who pass that we are the same as them in our earthly clothes (hence Ivor wears his suit) and then they are not frightened by any angelic beings before they begin their unexpected (to them) spiritual journeys. Although the dear ones, whom we rescue, do not believe in Jesus, He believes in them and is always there, in all His radiance, to give them His Love and His Blessing at the final stage of their journey when they 'see the light' and know that they are safe. What a blessing that must be!

I should point out that although we help many people to go through the light, we are never asked to help those who have committed heinous crimes, such as murder etc. against humanity and all life on the earth plane, without the right motive. These people are taken separately to another place. All I can say is although they think they have escaped justice on the earth plane, they will never escape it in the afterlife, and will regret for evermore the sins they have committed.

When a partner dies in a relationship it is so very hard for the person left behind to pick up the threads and continue with their lives. Luckily, we had been carrying out soul rescues and other spiritual service all our lives since we married in 1979, and so I was well versed in spiritualism when Ivor passed in 2015, and knew that I would see him again when once I passed myself – we are soul mates and our love bond can never be broken.

For others who don't understand and think that their dear one is lost to them forever, I cannot imagine the despair they must feel, so please, please know that your loved ones are not lost. Once they go through the light (of their own accord or with help) they are taken maybe, if needed, to a resting place (if they have suffered a long illness) and then, once recovered they will then join their partners and their loved ones, friends, etc. who have passed before them, and will have a wonderful reunion. After this they will start to live once again. As soon as they go through the light they will return to their prime – early twenties maybe – and be fit and well once again in their light bodies. Just imagine: no arthritis or other illnesses, and no old age – wonderful. They will be able to dance, play games, even swim in an ocean but never get wet, do whatever they want to, but, best of all, they will be with their loved ones.

I cannot tell you how wonderful the afterlife is – the colours are unimaginable, and the trees, flowers, parkland etc. unbelievable, but please no shortcuts. Live your life fully in this world; don't leave the dear ones you leave behind with pain and suffering, and sometimes guilt. Endure your life whatever it takes, then afterwards you can enjoy the pleasures of your new one!

Back to my story again, looking back on our life together it does seem unbelievable that we were able to achieve what we did, but I keep reminding myself that we did take 36 years to complete it. It was necessary for us to do all the tasks we did to enable us to live here – we certainly didn't have the money to hire people to do them for us at that time. Everything Ivor did was given the maximum of thought and the minimum of energy, and how true the saying, 'Necessity is the mother of invention.'

We now realise that everything was very carefully managed for us to be able to live at Millcroft Bungalow – an ideal location for our spiritual work and a beautiful place for us to live – by the agricultural lease being attached to the bungalow, making it a much cheaper proposition for us to afford to buy. In the end, although we had extra work to do to fulfil the conditions of the lease, i.e. to plant cider apple trees in the field and grow chrysanthemums and all it entailed in the acre attached to the bungalow, neither task was very onerous, but what would we have done without the terrific help of Sue and John in the beginning!

When we retired from our jobs with the Ministry, we also retired from the lease. I was extremely lucky last year, with the tremendous help of Paul, my son-in-law, together with an expert on land and estate management, to appeal to the district council for the removal of the agricultural lease and all its conditions, and was successful. What a relief!

As I have said before, right from the start of buying Millcroft Bungalow in 1979 we held some lovely family parties and have the photographs to prove it, but how I miss all my dear family that have now passed – everyone was precious! I always regretted that Mum and Dad were not still alive to be able to join in all the fun we had; they would have loved seeing us all together, enjoying ourselves, which of course they have now been able to do so 'from afar'. We were told, by a medium a few years after we moved into Millcroft, that it had been destined for us to live here thousands of years ago. Our comment was that we wish we had known that at the time when we were worrying and having so much difficulty in fulfilling all the obligations to be able to do so, and thinking that it would never happen. They must have thought, 'There's gratitude for you.'

I must now express my gratitude to my neighbours Arthur and Frances (now deceased) and John (also for all his caring during lockdown) who made it possible for us to live in this lovely bungalow, to dear Francine for always being there when I need her, to my good friend Ruth, and many more for their unfailing help and kindness over the years.

I have been very lucky all my life, having had a very loving and close family around me. I have also some lovely nieces and nephews whom I love dearly, and in particular, Sara and Karen for visiting me so many times in hospital to keep my spirits up, and in so many other ways. I had two good marriages and a wonderful daughter, Jane, together with two beautiful granddaughters, Julia, a nurse, and Laura, an accountant (now living in the Cayman Islands) from Jane's marriage to John, and a lovely extended family from Jane's marriage to Paul, my dear son-in-law. Now, one of my granddaughters Laura, (who is now married to David) has produced my first great grandchild, dear little Jack, and because I am now the proud owner of a 'smart' mobile phone,

I can follow his progress almost from day to day by courtesy of dear Laura and David on WhatsApp, so what more can I ask?

I have also to thank the Dawlish Christian Spiritualist Church for all the wonderful times I have spent there. I love the hymns that we sing, the little choir that I am a member of, the prayers that are said from the heart, the philosophy and the beautiful comforting messages that we receive from our loved ones in spirit realm. I am also very thankful for all the dear friends (too many to mention) I have made, including dear Jo and Ian, the president and secretary, and for the comfort of spiritualism which has made my life complete, and I thank God for it.

Sheila Hutchings
May 23, 2020

MORE MEMORIES OF THE WAR AND OUR LIVES AT ROCK COTTAGE AND RIVER VIEW

My childhood at Rock Cottages, Milbury Lane, Exminster, included the start of the war for me, having been born in 1933 and the war beginning in 1940. Looking back on it now I am so pleased that I was only seven years old and didn't really understand the terrible things that were happening in our world as so many countries fell under Nazi rule, and terrible atrocities took place, especially the one that befell the Jewish community. It wasn't until much later that we learnt exactly what had happened to the tragic Jews, and then of course, much later again when we saw the

111

unbelievable horror camps that a lot of them ended their lives in. Our prayers were sorely needed then.

The President of our little Dawlish Christian Spiritualist Church (before Ian) told me about his experience in the army when his battalion had to go into one of the camps, Belsen, to repatriate the dear ones, and said that this was one experience he would never ever forget, and one that I never want to remember after he explained what horrors he was subjected to.

Yes, we heard something of what was going on in the war on our old wireless, but as I said, most of it went over my head, but I remember later when I was about ten years old and was taken to the cinema I slowly slipped under the seat watching the Pathe newsreel in sheer terror, trying to get away from looking at all the rows and rows of the German Army, watched over by Hitler and his Gestapo friends, marching or goose-stepping to harsh discordant music being loudly played, as I was so frightened that they would come and capture us all. Thankfully, I had dear Dad to explain to me that nobody was coming, that Churchill and his team would save us in our hour of need, (he was very patriotic) and that we were lucky to have them and all the other brave men and women fighting for the 'cause' (and he was quite right). I wasn't quite sure what the 'cause' was but I soon found out when our sweets and chocolates were rationed and you had to have coupons for every stitch of clothing you wanted to buy (not that we had too much money to buy stitching of any sort!) but of course the cause was to beat Hitler and save all the other poor countries that had fallen foul of him, freedom for all.

When we received our gasmasks we had a lot more evidence of the war descending on us rapidly. When we all tried them on it certainly brought it home to us all how imminent the war was becoming and although there was a lot of laughing at each other, trying to bump our long noses together, the rubbery smell of them was overwhelming – I can smell it now – and seeing the blackout material on the table ready for Mum to make into curtains made it even more so. Thank goodness we never had to use them, the gasmasks I mean – we certainly had to use the blackout curtains!!

Every news film showed the destruction that was taking place all over the world, in every country, and soon it was happening to us, in our little village (in a fairly small way thank goodness) but we soon got used to the sirens going off quite frequently to warn us that an air raid was imminent, and as we had a RAF Camp with radar located in the village close by the River Exe at the end of Station Road, I soon learnt that this was a potential target for the 'jerries' and they certainly had a go at trying to hit the camp, but thankfully and extremely amazing for us, because River View was not very far away from the camp, they didn't succeed, although we had a bomb fall in a field at the back of Exminster Hill not very far from us, and I remember going to see the crater much later on!

The war became very real for us too when we heard that Plymouth and Exeter were bombed and the devastation was terrible – all the buildings razed to the ground into just piles of rubble. We saw all this on '*Pathe Newsreels*' in the cinemas and in the newspapers, and, of course, heard about it on our old wireless set – no telly then). We had two dear friends who told us that they were air raid wardens on duty on the roof of the Co-op in Exeter that night and said that as fast the incendiary bombs were dropping, they had to grab them and throw them over the side of the building. Just imagine it. What a nightmare.

Ivor used to tell the story that when he was about 12 years old his mother and father took him to visit his brother who was on national service at the time in a camp in Looe, Cornwall, and they were walking along the sea front when his father heard someone say to another person, 'It's a lovely night, yes, and those jerries will take advantage and be over for sure later.' With that, his father said, 'Come on, we're not waiting for the late train, we're going to go home now,' and they got a move on and managed to catch an earlier one. His father always liked to get into the front carriages of the train but as they were full up they had to go further back. As they were drawing into Newton Abbot Station the 'jerries' arrived and their train received a direct hit, and the first three carriages were blown to smithereens. Their carriage escaped luckily but he said there was so much glass around that they all received cuts but, they managed to jump down from the train and his father made them all run to the park and take shelter, away from the devastation. Ivor said he had never been so frightened in his life, and saw some terrible sights, but they got home safely.

Back to our life at Rock Cottages: Dad made a chickens' run and he also built some rabbit pens in an old shed that we inherited, in the garden of Rock Cottage, so we were self-sufficient in rabbit and chicken meat, and also when we moved to River View. Dad also grew wonderful vegetables in the allotment (now the cemetery) and I spent many happy hours with him digging and raking. We made many friends in the allotments and a dear old chap gave me a lovely mother-of-pearl penknife which I treasured for years.

As I said before, our life in Rock Cottages, was idyllic, every child's dream where we were so happy, and with the added pleasure of a field at the back of our cottage where hay was made every year, with piles of hay bales left for us to play on (or so we thought) climbing all over them to our hearts' content! There was also a lovely big chestnut tree that we all used to climb – all gone now as there is a big housing estate (Gissons) in its place. There were the four of us children, and baby Gladys, living in the two-bed roomed cottage at Milbury Lane. We had a double bed – Edna and Margaret slept at the top and I slept with Barbara at the bottom, and the baby slept with Mum and Dad.

Luckily, we were all young at the time – I was seven when we moved to River View – and the highlight of my memories looking back to Rock Cottage was when Edna produced a pack of playing cards (after we had all said our prayers and were all nicely tucked up in bed by Mum to go to sleep) and played 'Snap' and 'Jack out of Doors', which was my favourite – four for the Ace, three for the King, two for the Queen and one for the Jack. We loved it until Mum twigged what we were up to and promptly put out the light (especially if it was school the next day) but somehow we managed to have our 'illicit' nights quite a few times, and it was thanks to these wonderful card evenings that the famous sayings 'not muchy good' and 'one for his knob' (his knob being the Jack – we didn't play Rummy) were created, and the sayings being repeated over and over again when playing card games with Julia and Laura (my grandchildren much later in life). I vividly remember those evenings, listening to the wind and rain outside and feeling happy and safe inside.

Every Sunday evening was bath night, after listening to *Itma* or *In Town Tonight*, lovely programmes on our old wireless set. Dad would fetch in the old tin bath hanging up outside (no, not the one we used for our ski slope in the quarry, but not much better as I remember, but certainly had no holes in it) and it was placed in front of the fire, and then it was all hands on deck. The youngest would go first, that was me at five years old – Gladys, as the baby (she would have been two years old) would have had her bath in the sink – and Mum would wash me all over with lovely scented soap (I always remember the smell of that soap – no, not carbolic!!!) I think the hot water was supplied from a large saucepan on the kitchen range and after it was emptied would be promptly filled up again (don't forget, this water had to be pumped) and placed back on the range (the range was the bane of Mum's life – it had to be black leaded every week). Dad would be waiting with a towel – and then it was Barb's turn, then Marg's and lastly Ed who was old enough to be left alone to wash herself!

Mum and Dad had theirs' when we went to bed! It was quite a ritual but we loved it. Dad was very witty, keeping us laughing the whole time, and singing silly songs. Working at the hospital with all his workmates he used to come home with very funny jokes, and his favourite was 'Don't come down that ladder George, I've taken it away'. There were several others that I can't remember (and there is no-one now that I can ask!) but we always laughed like drains every time Dad told them. Although we had a bathroom at River View I so missed our bath nights at Rock Cottages!

On the mornings of our birthdays we were permitted the honour of choosing two bottles of Corona, the colour being our own choice, and then pouring it into half a dozen cups, but I always remember it was always difficult to wash the colour out of the cups afterwards – the red and yellow corona was the worst – but even in my little mind then, I wondered what the corona was doing to our tummies! Later on, on the day of our birthdays, we always had a party and I remember we had delicious food (before the war) but Margaret, for some unknown reason, preferred bread and butter to anything else, and became well known for it – in fact Mum used to say to her before she went to any tea party – 'Don't eat all the bread and butter' but I recall our birthday parties were always popular with our friends – plenty to eat, as well as bread and butter – and playing smashing games like hunt the parcel, musical chairs, etc, etc.

The sweet rations made a huge difference in the war – we children couldn't wait for it to end when we could enjoy a full bar of chocolate instead of having to share it, and because of the rationing, and scarcity of food, we had no fruit whatsoever, except for the apples, pears and plums that were grown in season, and I remember when we were at River View, our dear neighbour made us some 'bananas' made with cooked parsnips and banana flavouring. They were awful but she would insist on watching us eating them and we all nearly choked trying to keep the 'bananas' in our mouths and saying how nice they were before we rushed out the door, without her knowing, to get rid of the awful banana substitute. As Mum said, 'She meant well!'

At the time we had some very funny songs that soon became popular on the wireless like 'We're going to hang out the washing on the Seigfried Line, have you any dirty washing mother dear?' 'Kiss me goodnight Sergeant Major, tuck me in my little wooden bed' 'Roll out the Barrel, we'll have a barrel of fun, Roll Out the Barrel, we'll have the huns on the run' etc, etc., which helped to take the seriousness out of the war for a short time, and, of course, all the various propaganda programmes on the wireless ridiculing Hitler and his huns to keep everybody's spirits up, and someone called Lord Haw Haw, but he was spreading propaganda for the other side!

We had a wonderful time playing outdoors in all the hedges at Rock Cottages. The farmers must have loved us (I don't think!) because we hollowed out every one to make shops of different kinds – fish and chips was the most popular with Mum's old ladle and a biscuit tin for the fryer, then followed the bakers, and then last of all the sweet shop. In the early days when we were very young (I must have been about five – there were two years between the first four children) Ed was in charge of the fryer because she was the eldest (and of course the fryer was very hot!) with large leaves for the fish and smaller ones for the chips. We pinched some of the newspaper from the outside privy to wrap them up. It was our job to cut it up into small squares, with a string to hang on a nail behind the door, so we felt we were entitled! Nobody seemed to mind except perhaps, on reflection, the poor chap using the privy! Barb was in charge of the cake shop and Marg liked serving all the sweets that she lusted after and could never afford at Cocky Diamond's. I remember she always took so long in telling us what she had on the shelves to sell – all lies and very boring. I was the youngest so I was the customer and had to do what I was told, so I had to listen, but I still remember those days with so much love and affection, and we still continued playing those games at River View, ruining once again a perfectly good hedge for our shopping enterprises!

When it was raining outside, and to keep us quiet, Mum would set the chairs up like seats in a bus. Usually I was the conductor, with one of Mum's handbags over my shoulder. Barb was the driver with a large plate for the steering wheel. Glad (being the youngest) was the passenger with dolls and stuffed animals occupying all the seats, and we usually enjoyed the ride until one of us, usually Glad, wanted to be the conductor instead and refused to pay her fare! Of course it didn't help that I refused to give up the handbag!

We also had Mum's larder to play with and took out all the packets of everything we could find to 'sell', with a cord Mum had hooked up to the picture rails, together with a cup dangling from it to put the money and receipts in, very similar to the money cable that the Co-op had at one time – before all the tills arrived. Of course, our system was so much better, although the cord did keep breaking when an enthusiastic saleswoman, mainly Barb, (never me of course) pulled the cord extra hard and broke it and the cup as well!

We always had lovely Christmases. We had an afternoon making paper chains – there were no decorations in the shops – not that we could afford anyway – and afterwards picked holly and ivy from the quarry. Mum always made a Christmas cake and Christmas puddings (I still have Mum's recipes that I follow religiously every Christmas).

We always had a pillowcase full of toys each (how did she manage it?) We also had a big Christmas tree and we all took part in decorating it. I remember going to the post office with Mum and buying some Father Xmas lights for the tree. I am still the proud owner of one of them! When we arrived home, we were surprised and delighted to find that we had two sets in one box!

When we were younger, especially at Rock Cottages, Dad used to go out and ring some bells on Christmas Eve, and we were always taken in by him and raced to get into bed before father Christmas came because some of us were a little bit frightened in case we should see him, and in fact we nearly did when one Christmas Eve, Dad tiptoed into the bedroom with our toys early in the morning and tripped over somebody's slippers, and it was not a very nice word that Father Christmas uttered under his breath – I know because I heard him! When we got older Mum said that was the last time she allowed him to be Father Christmas's 'little helper'!

There was something else magical in my life at that time and I think the thing I missed the most when we left Rock Cottages was a beautiful little stream running alongside the lane, and I used to love playing in it with my shoes off as it had a lovely sandy bottom, and I caught tadpoles in a jar and made little dams and small waterfalls. That stream was truly magic. It had a tunnel at the end leading into a field and Barb, Glad and I used to love making paper boats and seeing which one came out first at the end of the tunnel. How I loved that stream and it was solely ours, or most times, not like Berrybrook which was too popular with the locals!

Clothes were always in short supply during the war and jumble sales at that time were very popular. I was privileged to wear several of the dresses made for my friend Jean, by her aunt and which I inherited when they became too small for her (the niece I mean). Although I was the same age as her, I was taller but much thinner (like a rake they always said) so although the skirts were a little short, I had ample room to grow into the tops, but I loved them, especially a lovely pink and white polka-dot creation that had a big bow on the back, a lovely dress which I was very proud to wear, in fact I was proud to wear all of them, and I was very grateful to Jean's mother for passing them on.

I was also given some lovely clothes by a very smart girl Joan who was a daughter of one of our neighbours. (Their little boy Paul – only five years old – had died of diphtheria, very sad, and had been in my class at the time.) The clothes were really lovely, very modern, and as I was attending the South Devon Technical College at the time I was extremely grateful for them, as Glad was when she could sneak them out of my wardrobe, but I never minded!

I don't know how Mum managed it but she always provided delicious meals for us but we still had our likes and dislikes. I hated cabbage but luckily I always had Glad sitting beside me to pass on my helping as, being the fair-minded person I was, I always gave her a roast potato as well as an added incentive. Most times this little transaction would go without a hitch; nobody being any the wiser on a good day, least of all Mum, but Glad had a mean streak in her. Sometimes she would move her plate to one side whilst the transfer was taking place and the dreaded cabbage would end up on the table – no tablecloths in those days – or, if she was feeling really mean (or I conveniently forgot to give her the roast potato more likely) she would let out a shout, 'Mum, she's put her cabbage on my plate again.' I don't know what I hated the most when she did that – the cabbage or her – but I always got a clipped ear from Mum for not eating the revolting green mess, together with the same boring old maxim, oft repeated by Mums the world over, 'Eat it up. The poor starving children in Africa would be glad to have it.' Under my breath I would always want to say 'Let 'em 'ave it then' but more often than not I kept quiet, in case I got another clip around the ear, but would be inwardly laughing as Glad would get her come-uppance by also getting a clip for being a snitch.

That was family life but I loved it and did I miss it when I left to get married! Glad and I were always arguing, especially when she pinched my clothes to wear behind my back. Dear Shirley was always the mediator, but I expect Glad had the same trouble later with her!!!

To supplement the rations in the war I remember queuing at Oaklands, a house at the bottom of River View, to buy some very tasty pasties. The owner of Oaklands was well-known in the village and also owned a business in Exeter which sold all manner of things very similar to W H Smith now, but of course not quite so big! Our family then became almost a 'cottage industry' and helped to produce silver leaves and other decorative items for weddings by pressing them out of large silver sheets of paper, We were also coaxed by Mum, to help the war effort, by making fishing nets and had large wooden 'needles' and enormous balls of green coarse twine, to handle (I think for camouflage nets) not to mention doing our bit by knitting socks for our brave fighting men out of dozens of balls of khaki wool, and they had to be brave to wear my socks with the heels I produced because I just couldn't get them right at all, but luckily Mum was always at hand to take over when I, with the best will in the world, tried but couldn't master the art, but I did improve vastly when I got older and surprisingly made some lovely cable stitch jumpers for Jane and Jack (with not a heel in sight!)

Edna and Margaret had steady boyfriends in their lives at the time the Americans arrived on the scene, around about 1943–44 – Barb and I were too young, thank goodness, for any shenanigans! Edna met a wounded soldier at the hospital (there were several wards given over to war casualties) and he became quite a regular visitor to our home. He was very nice but we all preferred Bill (same name) whom she eventually married.

Barb and I went two or three times to the museum with Auntie Milly (who was a member of the Exeter Women's Guild) when they held social nights for the Americans, and we helped to serve refreshments. (Ivor told me that he used to go there at that time as well with his mother, who used to belong to the Exeter 'Women's Voluntary Service' (WVS) – small world!) The Americans were always very polite and friendly and we enjoyed the evenings very much.

When we first arrived at River View, Mum made friends with all the neighbours and before long the youngest of us – Barbara and I to begin with, and then Gladys and Shirley, followed in our footsteps – were running errands for them, and every Saturday morning saw us going to the shops with one of Mum's handbags for the money, and taking the pushchair with a large bag (Mum had made of hessian) and a long list. We used to take it in turns sitting in the pushchair and having a ride on the way to the shops, and used to walk in the road on the way back – the pushchair was too heavy to get onto the pavement – good job there were not too many cars around at the time, being wartime and petrol rationing, but I do remember one day falling foul of a cyclist as we turned into our road in front of him, causing him to fall off. His language was appalling for such a small boy!!!

Another time Barb wanted to find out what vinegar tasted like on the way home. She soon found out after taking a big swig and then being violently sick in the gutter. I managed to put the top back on again afterwards and we never did find out what was said when the person who had paid good money for the vinegar, found the bottle half empty!

We always used to do our shopping at the Misses Gush's shop which is the large shop opposite the school. It was magic and had everything, food wise (more variety than Cocky Diamond's) but the entrance was always a bit difficult to manoeuvre, or I should say the exit when we had to manage the big bag to go home, but one of the Misses Gush was quite strong and would lift it onto the pushchair for us. She was a very kind lady and she often used to give us a lollipop each for our trouble, although I used to think (at naughty times) that a bar of chocolate, or even two, wouldn't have gone amiss for all the business we were giving her!

We had quite a number of shops at that time in the village. There was Lowes' Stores in the middle of the village selling lovely cheese and various cold meats kept under glass domes, and other delicious delicacies – I am sure that they were the pioneers of the modern delicatessens!

Auntie Dor, Uncle Joe, Dulcis, Walter and Gordon used to live in a little cottage (now pulled down) opposite, and I often used to go to the shop on an errand for Mum and stopped on the way home for a cup of tea with them. Uncle Joe (who was at sea in the navy during the war) from time to time brought home some lovely curios, amongst them lovely coloured glass ornaments which I loved and envied, and remember becoming very anxious when the children picked them up to play with. I believe they all survived! (The ornaments and the children!)

I nearly forgot to mention the old vicarage and, of course, our Sunday school trips. The vicarage was situated in the main road before you entered Milbury Lane. It is now a rest home (I believe) and a new vicarage has been built at the entrance to the churchyard. The old vicarage had lovely grounds, very accessible to the village, and many fetes were held there on the lawn, and I loved the lucky dip barrels and hoopla stalls, amongst other numerous attractions. Charabancs also departed from the old Vicarage every summer to take us, the Sunday school children, and our parents to the seaside where we could play and swim in the sea in the mornings and later take part in a sports afternoon with egg and spoon races, one-legged races, etc. organised by the Vicar.

We used to go to Goodrington mostly but also to Teignmouth and Paignton which had piers and with a lot of penny machines to play on. The pier was made up of big wooden planks that didn't quite marry up and left nasty cracks for your money to drop through – if you had any to drop! We used to save up our pennies to spend on such an occasion but Margaret always seemed to have more than anyone else on the day. It figured really as she was the only sensible one amongst us who, instead of spending all her money on sweets, kept some for a rainy (most times it was) day, and I always noticed that she always had a handful left to take home when we had lost every single one!

Mrs Brands' shop was also a grocery store, next door to the Stowey Arms, at the top of the village, and just above Mrs Brands was the shoe repair shop.

The shoe repairer didn't get too much business from our family – Dad had his own metal 'shoe' and some old leather belts he used to repair our shoes with. They were a bit heavy at times when he finished, but it did the job and were much better than some of the boots the boys had to wear to school, with cardboard in the soles, or some of the thin-soled silver or gold dance shoes the girls had to endure, as they had to in the war when they had nothing else. Luckily (or unluckily), there were a lot of poor families living in the village at that time (us for a start) and everyone was in the same boat so no-one stared or passed any comment, it was the norm, although, on the odd occasion, high heels worn by the thirteen-year-olds caused quite a stir, if only amongst the teachers!

Halfway down the village was Mac's store, a kind of a cabin that sold sweets, cigarettes, ice-cream etc (opposite where the garage is now) and was very handy because it opened on Sundays.

Scagells the butcher was opposite Limes Cottages before it was taken over by Gerald and his 'little alf'. Another member of the Gush family owned the paper shop opposite Victory Hall, and delivered our daily paper. The policeman's house was next door – his son used to go to our school – with the post office almost opposite. I have already told you about 'our' shop in Milbury Lane!

As I said before, I often used to go and stay with Auntie Milly and Uncle Ralph, and one day Barb was also asked if she would like to go too, and for a treat Auntie Milly took us for a walk in the fields at the back of where she lived (Stoke Hill Estate is built there now). We had started picking up fir cones for Auntie Milly's fire when all at once I decided that I wanted to have a wee. Auntie Milly came with me and we went behind the hedge when all at once someone started to throw cones at us. Several actually, and frightened us out of our wits – good job I was relieving myself or there could have been a nasty accident! Auntie Milly became very indignant and started to shout, 'Hey, what's going on?' whereupon Barb's little face appeared above the hedge holding the handles of the bag of cones that we had painstakingly picked up saying, 'Sorry, sorry, they came off in me and', meaning the handles. Of course, she had been twisting the bag of cones above her head when the handles gave way. How we laughed and I never let her forget it.

We all had our various tasks to do in the home, some good, some not so good, but we always believed that ours was one of the worst when we had to go to the nurseries down the road to pull the 'milkydashels' (our name for them) in all winds and weather! Dad had very 'kindly' arranged for us to perform this task every week to help the nurseries keep the weeds down, and for us to feed the rabbits. We had to take some sacks with us and bring them back full. This was not one of our favourite pastimes so we were more than relieved when Dad decided to put an end to the rabbits once and for all and concentrate on the chickens! I never did like the fur gloves very much anyway!

It was after the war that Edna had her 21st birthday, and I remember Mum giving the postman a glass of sherry for bringing masses of cards for Edna, and all the neighbours gave her lovely presents. (She was very popular, and of course they all knew us for running their errands). She had a party in the Victory Hall and Mum, Edna, Margaret and Barbara did the refreshments and I remember Dad had ordered barrels of beer and cases of wine. We had a real celebration (we all seemed to be ready for it) but it was nothing like her wedding when a lady in the village made her wedding dress and I believe seven bridesmaids' dresses, in four different colours. She was a very clever lady and all the dresses were lovely. Mine was pale green I believe, and I loved it. It was the first long dress I had ever had, apart from the crinoline I wore as carnival queen – although I had another long dress in lilac which I loved when I was a bridesmaid for Barb's wedding to Roy, which was another lovely occasion with the reception in the Victory Hall.

Talking about long dresses, I was always envious when I used to see Edna, Margaret and Barbara dressing up to go to the annual New Year's Ball at the hospital. They always looked stunning.

Ed and Marg had beautiful naturally curly hair whereas Barb, Glad and I had hair straight as candles, as we used to say. Ed and Marg's was dark brown in colour, Barb's was ginger which turned to a lovely auburn when she got older, I was mouse brown and Glad was blonde. Shirley had brown curly hair (as did Johnny although I don't think his was curly come to think of it) and Mike's was fair but straight. The joke in the family was there were obviously many different milkmen at that time in the village. Mum was not amused!!!

Mum treated me to a perm when I was carnival queen. For once I had lovely thick curly hair. How I loved it, and I have loved perms ever since, costing me a fortune all my life. How I envied Margaret and Edna their beautiful naturally curly hair.

As life progresses and we all get older, inevitably we must accept that we all have to pass (or die) at some time or another, but it was a terrible shock when we lost Mum but not quite so much when we lost Dad, although we were still heartbroken. He was 78 years of age, when he passed and was ready to go and be rid of all his aches and pains, and of course, wanting so much to be with Mum as I now know that he is, but it was another terrible shock when we lost dear Ian, a wonderful young lad of only 17 years of age, and it was, once again, a devastating tragedy for all the family. He was with his best friend when they were both killed in a car crash, travelling home from their 'Passing-out parade' as marine cadets. Shirley (his mother) and Chris (her second husband) were staying with us at the time and it was devastating to have to tell her that they had died. We all attended their funeral, conducted by the Royal Marines with all the honours they could bestow upon them.

Although Ivor and I were informed a long time ago, when we first began our spiritual journey, that when we are born, we have a date also for our passing (good job we don't know it), we all have to go at our allotted time, and evidently, so we are told, if dear Ian and friend hadn't been killed in that accident, they would have died anyway on that specific day in some other way. Pity the poor driver of that fatal car.

As I have said previously, it was a terrible blow when all my dear sisters and brother died when they did – I still miss them all terribly but I know that they are now all very happy and enjoying their new lives, together with Mum and Dad and all our other dearest relatives.

Our life at River View was a little different to our life at Milbury Lane, at least for Dad who was now in his element, having a boy to go fishing with and someone with whom he could discuss football, cricket, golf, etc, etc. that he never could with us girls. Their interest in fishing even led to dear

Mum being coaxed to join them on a rare visit to the canal banks, and often Jack, Jane and I would be persuaded to take a walk to the pond in station road to give them their egg sandwiches and see Dad and John in action, catching two fish (or maybe even four) after many long hours of trying – but were they happy!

A great advantage in being at River View was the electrical lighting and eventually a tap with running water (not a pump) and a flush toilet. There was a bathroom, a coal fire in the living room and an electric stove to cook on, but I look back to Rock Cottages with so much love and affection for all the drawbacks, i.e. bitter cold winters with just the coal range and paraffin stoves to keep us warm, oil lamps to see by, no running water, only the pump outside, and toilets at the end of our row of cottages, but I loved my life in both homes, thanks to dear Mum and Dad and all my lovely sisters and brothers that made it so good, and I wouldn't have changed one minute of it, but my life at River View came to an end when I married Jack and said goodbye to my family, and how I missed them. Glad was 17 years old, Shirley 14, Johnny 10 and Michael 2.

Mum loved children. How sad she must have been to see all of us leave the nest, one by one – she always kept food on the table in case one of us dropped by!

After I left and had Jane, I used to bring her home to River View on the 'bus and she played with Mike, as well as Lynne, and they all grew up together, and they have been close ever since. One year, when Mike was about 15 years old he came with us to Butlins, and I was thrilled when he won a small amount of money on a game of bingo.

I hated leaving them all behind but I know that life, although hard for them at times, was a happy one, and that they all looked back at their home life with much love and affection, and gratitude to have had such loving parents as our Mum and Dad.

Sheila Hutchings
May 23, 2020

Ingram Content Group UK Ltd.
Milton Keynes UK
UKHW021514220623
423876UK00009B/157